I Witness

Ray
Kostulias

I Witness

Dramatic Monologues
from Hebrew Scriptures

United Church Press   Cleveland, Ohio

United Church Press, Cleveland, Ohio 44115
© 1997 by Ray Kostulias

All rights reserved. Published 1997

Printed in the United States of America on acid-free paper

02 01 00 99 98 97   5 4 3 2 1

Library of Congress Cataloging-in-Publication Data

Kostulias, Ray, 1947–
    I witness : dramatic monologues from Hebrew Scriptures /
Ray Kostulias.
       p. cm.
    ISBN 0–8298–1175–3 (pbk. : alk. paper)
    1. Bible O.T.—History of Biblical events—Drama. 2. Bible
plays, American. 3. Monologues. I. Title.
PS3561.08434I2   1997
812'.54—DC21   96–51942
                                            CIP

In memory of Peter, my father.

Contents

Acknowledgments

For assistance, advice, and encouragement, I am grateful to: Jeanne Sabatie, Rabbi Phillip Berkowitz, Dr. John Danner, Madelyn and Len Levy, Marjani Dele, and the members of First Congregational Church, UCC, Park Ridge, New Jersey.

Introduction

The most commonly asked question in response to the dramatic monologues I have written and performed is: "Are they factual?" My reply is: "To a point." The characters and situations I portray are solidly based on the available evidence in each case, but, invariably, at some *point*, reliable information runs out and conjecture takes over. This is not a bad thing. Imagination provides vitality in our engagement with Scripture. It operates upon the text naturally and inevitably, as much for literalists as for liberals, whether resisted or indulged. Regardless of theological stance, when we read the Bible we *all* fill in the blanks! The more consciously we do so, the more faithful to the original we are likely to be.

Divine revelation encompasses human creativity. The Word of God is more than words—more than a compilation of wise sayings and philosophical principles, however profound and beneficial these might be; more than an appeal to intellectual assent, as important as that is. The Word of God intends to grip us— heart, mind, and soul; emotion, reason, and imagination—so that no one part of being can overrule faith for the other parts. The Spirit seeks wholeness. Our spirits seek wholeness. The spiritual quest, as always, and today more than ever, is about integration, a movement from abstraction to experience. We long to *feel* as well as to *know* God.

Drama, in its highest forms, connects feeling and knowledge. By definition, it strives for embodiment and, as such, can be a valuable tool for communicating multifaceted truth. Drama pleads for response: engaging dormant conscience, beleaguered faith, unrealized hope, rejected love; fomenting a spiritual rebellion of good against evil, life against death. It aims not only to persuade but to motivate, to be not only coherent but compelling.

Clearly, in practice, drama infrequently fulfills this sublime purpose—much like religion in this respect. But both retain an underlying power upon which their kinship is based. Both aim to instruct and inspire, to teach and transform.

Three elements of drama are particularly applicable to the task of proclaiming faith, by activating intellect and emotion.

1. Character

In the information age, the gathering of facts has become a consuming, if not obsessive, concern. Much of this data appears on computer screens and fax sheets, blares from stereo speakers, or crackles over cellular phone lines, providing us with the "benefit" of transacting daily business with a minimum of personal contact. We take the detached process for granted.

However, when it comes to *interpreting* the wealth—glut?—of information, we still rely on more intuitive methods. Usually, we filter it through personalities: politicians, commentators, consultants, celebrities, teachers, ministers, therapists, friends. In spite of all the technological magic that bypasses human interaction, people continue to learn from people.

Not just style but substance as well is involved. We believe the analysis of a certain news reporter because she impresses us as trustworthy. We dismiss the speech of a certain legislator because he strikes us as opportunistic. Undoubtedly there is danger in forming judgments on the basis of purely subjective reactions, but there is an equal danger in forming judgments solely on the basis of supposedly objective evidence which seldom reaches us in unedited form. We cannot escape the struggle to reconcile what is said with what we sense. That struggle defines us. It is our saving grace. Only by wrestling with the contradictions of the world can we grasp the unity of life. These contradictions and the spiritual growth they make possible are most often encountered in relationships.

How can we relate to the characters of the Bible who not only propose but often embody the divine message? We hear their words but we miss their feelings, expressions, gestures, body language, pained silences, bursts of exuberance—natural indicators of a personal investment in their universal statements. The solution, I believe, is in freeing our imaginations to re-create the emotions that must have enlivened their experience of God's reality. Fears, failures, doubts, memories, and hopes were for them, and are for us, a primary source of revelation.

Drama presents characters we can learn *with*, not just *from*. Acknowledging our connection with them, we intuit our common connection with the God who uses the richness of character to draw us closer to one another and to the Other.

2. Story

Notice how, in the midst of a didactic sermon, the attention of the congregation perks up when the preacher introduces an illustration. The promise of a plot line, dialogue, humor, complication, pathos, and surprise shifts the focus from left to right brain, from abstraction to interaction. In most preaching, however, illustrations play a "supporting" role, designed to "back up" theological points. They are usually prefaced with a specific interpretation ("This is what you should get from the story") and followed by a recapitulation of the predetermined message ("This is what you should have gotten from the story").

Drama takes the opposite approach, relying upon the inherent power of the story itself. Drama says, in effect, "Here is a slice of life. Enter in and exit with your own conclusions." Of course, a good playwright (or a good preacher using drama effectively) will suggest a direction for our thoughts and feelings. But too much instruction will make us lazy. No need to question when the answer is handed to us. No need to delve into our conflicting responses if one "proper" response is dictated to us.

Ironically, perhaps, it is *more* difficult to "follow" the straight line of a purely logical sermon than to "ride" the twists and curves of a logically pure story. Drama gives us room to roam among multiple meanings and various feelings and to claim for ourselves those that may empower our faith and improve our lives.

3. Suspense

Why would the Holy Spirit bother to intervene in situations where we insist on controlling the future? We *don't* anyway! The schemes and theories we develop in our attempts to manage life are blown apart every day, day after day, so much so that we would be led to despair had we no higher plan to which we could entrust our destiny. God does not expect us to predict or proscribe what *will be* but to observe and respond faithfully to what *is*, to act boldly in the present and trust bravely in God's future.

The worldly systems in which we are enmeshed dread such allegiance to a higher court and mock it with all the instruments of influence at their disposal. Too clever to condemn our deepest longings outright, they praise the *concept* of faith as long as it does not challenge our embrace of the status quo; they admire the *notion* of spirituality as long as it remains gloriously impractical. We are conditioned to accept the delusion of ultimate control over our own fate (which makes it easier for us to be exploited because our hardships appear to be the result of personal failure, quite apart from any form of systemic, societal injustice inflicted upon us).

Drama intentionally undermines this false sense of control by creating suspense, withholding resolution, veiling the outcome, subverting temporal authority, and raising our sights to an eternal scenario that we can neither predict or direct. Drama lures us into the unknown where we must wait for truth to take shape on its own terms. The uncertainty is frightening; but since this is our natural state of being, it is also exciting. We recognize ourselves in that mimetic limbo. And the reunion of those generally segregated emotions—of threat and thrill—produce awe, the essential condition for profound worship.

More and more, these days, both clergy and laity are rediscovering the power of drama and dramatic technique in worship, spiritual retreats, Bible study, religious education, mission, and evangelism. I hope these monologues will be helpful on this journey of faith.

Hagar

Genesis 16–17

I AM HAGAR, a servant, a concubine, a mother, an outcast. Abraham, "the father of the Hebrew people," was also the father of my son. I "belonged" to Sarah and she "gave" me to her husband when she believed she was barren. But when I had conceived the hoped-for child, she became jealous, and they sent me away. I have always been at the mercy of other peoples' plans, or change of plans. My life has always been controlled by other peoples' decisions.

I was born in Egypt, raised and educated in the court of the Pharaoh, which sounds like a fortunate, elegant upbringing; and it would have been for anyone with a royal pedigree, but not for me, an orphan of commoners. My parents died before I knew them, before I could form any memories of them, and I was taken to the palace for one purpose: to be trained as a slave, to learn to move quietly and efficiently through a setting of wealth and power and privilege, and to be part of the scenery.

In childhood, whatever we are forced to endure is "normal" to us. If we are mistreated, we try to avoid the pain as best we can, but we don't yet grasp that it's wrong, that it can be resisted, that it can be challenged, denied, cursed, and condemned. We adapt to what is because we have no other experience. I was taught to

1

do the bidding of my superiors and nearly everyone was my superior. I . . . adapted.

So, when the Pharaoh presented me as a gift to Sarah and Abraham, I couldn't conceive of a suitable objection. It seemed just another turn on the road I was meant to travel. The fear of leaving my homeland as the property of strangers remained unspoken, an unseen wound in my heart.

In those days, famine gripped the land. But the leaders of my country had been wise enough to store the excess from past harvests to see us through the lean years. And they were generous to our starving, nomad neighbors who streamed into the city of Thebes in a desperate search for food. In return, the Pharaoh received chariots, incense, gold, and copper—all the treasures that were useless to those with nothing to eat.

The famine brought Abraham to Egypt. He came in a great caravan, with a great company of his people, with goods to trade for corn and barley. But the Pharaoh was interested in another kind of trade, one that involved Abraham's "sister." Sarah *was* half-sister to Abraham. She was also his wife—a fact not mentioned in the negotiations. She was very beautiful and, to the eyes of an Egyptian, exotic—her features and complexion foreign enough to inspire a lust for novelty. The Pharaoh took notice. He desired her.

I understand how it happened. Between a prince and a petitioner, there is no balance of power. The ruler demands, takes, and silences argument. A *husband* is an obstacle who can be eliminated with a word of authority. But a *brother* can be placated, convinced, even rewarded for his deference to the passions of a king.

So, Abraham lied. Sarah assumed her false role. Pharaoh opened the granaries, and Hagar became the maidservant of his new mistress.

But secrets are seldom permanent. When, finally, the deception was exposed, the Pharaoh was torn between anger and guilt.

Perhaps he suspected the truth from the beginning. That would explain the leniency of the sentence he decreed. Banishment was hardly the most severe punishment under the circumstances. Abraham and Sarah were allowed to leave with their lives and their possessions—which now included me.

We set out across the desert in search of a new home and, after much traveling, settled at Hebron by the Oaks of Mamre where Abraham built an altar to his God.

As a girl in Egypt, I paid little attention to the gods of my people. If those divine beings took any interest in *human* beings, I had no evidence of it. To me, they were just names to sanctify the whims of those who had everything and wanted more. The gods of Egypt were careful not to contradict the will of their earthly masters.

The God of the Hebrews was different. This . . . Yah-weh . . . gave orders, made promises, offered guidance, demanded obedience. Even Abraham, whose word was our law, approached this God on his knees. When Abraham gathered us together to hear God's revelation, he spoke of a plan. The Covenant, he called it. An arrangement between earth and heaven. If we trusted in the God of Abraham, above all others, we would be provided with a homeland and a heritage forever.

We would be provided? For myself, it would be a secondhand blessing, at best. And yet, I was moved by the possibility of a God who could see through the disguises that separate the mighty from the lowly. A God who might care for a poor servant named Hagar.

Of course, I was not one of the chosen, not part of the family, but, in the beginning, it seemed that I was accepted and valued. Sarah treated me gently and even seemed to enjoy my company. Sometimes she'd have me sit beside her and comb her long, dark hair, then she'd talk to me, as if to a friend, about her hopes and disappointments.

Once I had the courage to ask if she shared her husband's trust in the God, Yahweh. She admitted that her faith rested more on

Abraham's unshakable belief than on any experience of her own. "It's enough," she said with a smile, "for one person in the family to have visions."

One of those visions caused her great pain. Abraham had been promised many descendants, as many as the stars that could be counted in the sky, but Sarah had not produced even one child.

When she cried, I kept silent. It was not proper for me to offer her comfort. But I felt her sorrow which, in a way, was similar to mine. I wondered what chance *I* had to hold a daughter or a son in my arms. Would I die lonely, with nothing to call my own and no one to remember me?

Though I had passed my twentieth birthday, I had never been with a man, had never felt anything close to the kind of love I imagined was necessary for marriage. Even among the Hebrews, there were young men who stared at me and tagged along after me as I went about my chores. But nothing permanent could be hoped for with them. One day, they would marry someone of their own race. In the meantime, I had no interest in being one of their boyhood adventures.

On the other hand, the thought of settling down with someone of my own station was just as depressing. Greeting each other in passing as we hurried on to our separate tasks—me with a bucket of laundry to take to the stream and he with a bucket of feed to take to the animals. Slumped over dinner at the end of the day, too tired to talk. Lying in bed, side by side, like two lumps of clay. Save me from this, O God!

Who did I hope would hear this prayer? I could not answer that very clearly, not even to myself. But I had begun to imagine a God with a heart, a Parent who named and cradled and cherished every child, who ached at our sadness, who wanted nothing more than our happiness, and who would never leave us. Was this the God called Yahweh? For now, that name would have to do.

When I hinted at my fears, Sarah told me not to worry. "You're young and strong. You will have a husband and many children. I wish we could trade places."

I believe the idea came to her the very moment when she spoke those words. After that, she sought me out more frequently and spoke more urgently of her distress. It was more than merely a personal tragedy for Sarah. She saw herself as the obstacle to the destiny of her people. "What was this God thinking?" she asked with a bitter smile. "Why choose me? Why not someone who can do the job? Why not someone like . . . you?"

Then, one day, she took the brush from my hand, told me to sit in her chair, and she began to brush my hair.

"I can see a child in this house," she said. "A son, healthy and beautiful. As precious as if he were my own. But not mine, yours. Your son, Hagar."

A feeling of dread washed over me. "I don't understand."

"Your son," she said. "We can raise him together. With two of us it will be so much easier. There's no reason why we can't solve this problem. A little human ingenuity to assist heaven's purpose. Abraham isn't so ancient that he can't be revived by a lovely young girl like you. You will bear his child, we will have an heir, and God's promise will be fulfilled after all."

"Please," I cried in terror. "Please don't ask me to do such a thing."

"I am not asking," she said. "It has already been arranged."

One thought sustained me during that time: the child will be mine and my child will never be surrendered. Not to Abraham's visions or Sarah's schemes. Ishmael will be *my* son!

Sarah must have read this fierce vow in my eyes. She turned cold and cruel, eager to detect the slightest signs of insolence or neglect on my part. More than anything, she was jealous. As my belly swelled, her temper grew shorter, her punishments more severe. She went to Abraham, told him that I looked upon her with contempt—which was not untrue. If there had ever been a bond between us, it was broken now. I continued to be the docile servant and kept my bitter feelings to myself. But nothing I did satisfied Sarah. Abraham had lost interest in me by then.

"She's your maid," he said. "Do to her as you please."

The fear of my mistress, the indifference of everyone around me, the uncertainty of my life became too much to bear. One morning before dawn, with no plan in mind, I simply ran away. I took what food and clothing I could carry and fled. Into the desert.

Foolish decision. In my condition, I couldn't go far without having to rest, and each time I stopped, it seemed harder to begin again. By midday, I had covered barely a few miles. The sun baked my skin and my throat was parched. I had not taken any water with me, assuming that before long I would come upon a stream or a village where I could ease my thirst. But the bleak landscape had not changed all day. I felt dizzy and weak. If not for the child within me, I would have sat on the ground and waited to die, but even in my despair, I could not deny him his chance for life. I found some shade under a tree and I prayed.

It was not the kind of humble, plaintive prayer you might expect. If God meant for us to perish on this road to nowhere, what use was it to beg for mercy? If God intended to rescue us, it was time to do so. If miracles were possible, I demanded one now.

I rose from my knees and my anger pushed me back onto the path. Almost immediately I saw it, just ahead. A well. It was old and overgrown, perhaps dried out ages ago. But with a surge of hope I stumbled toward it as quickly as my trembling legs would take me. Moments later, I was gulping down cold, clear water, tipping the bucket over my head to soak my body, laughing and crying at the same time. For all the pain in the world, life doesn't give up easily.

My body had been refreshed, but my mind still raced in confusion. I closed my eyes and tried to imagine where we would be tomorrow. I saw myself in a familiar house, at a table, kneading dough for bread. My infant baby played on the floor beside me. Suddenly, he got to his feet and became a husky child. He turned to me and he was taller. He came closer and I saw the adolescent stubble of a beard on his cheeks. He reached out with a muscular arm, took my hand, and said, "Mother, I'm a man now."

Sarah entered the room. "Ishmael," she said. "There's work to be done." She stared at me and said, "Hurry up with that bread."

"No!" I said aloud, opening my eyes. "I can't go back. I will die there."

"Or die here, in the desert, and your son will never be born."

It was a dialogue in my head. *"I will lose him. They will take him from me."*

"No! He has a separate destiny, and you will live to see it. It has been promised. I have promised it."

A feeling of peace flowed through my body. A gentle breeze blew across my face. At my feet, a bright pink flower I hadn't noticed before seemed to have blossomed just for this moment. I picked it and breathed in its fragrance. I was still unsure of the answer, but I knew I had received it. I stepped onto the road and headed back to my old life. But somehow I knew that I would never be the same. I had heard the voice of God.

The years passed quickly. My son grew up healthy and strong, and he became the whole purpose of my life. I comforted him when he was sad, I listened to his dreams, I taught him to be proud, to bow to no one, for he was the heir to the Covenant. The *only* heir.

But when Ishmael was thirteen years old, all my plans for him were threatened. Abraham had had another vision. Yahweh commanded that every male among us should be circumcised. It came to me as a rumor and when I first heard it, I laughed. Surely this was not God's idea. Life itself provides us with more then enough scars. We needn't inflict them on ourselves.

Then, Abraham made the announcement: "It will be a sign of faithfulness for all generations. Every male child, eight days old, and all other males, boys and men, will undergo the ritual."

At first I felt nothing but defiance. *You will not do this thing to my son*! But my determination was soon replaced by a feeling of helplessness. If Ishmael was to be included in the Covenant and receive his inheritance, he could not refuse to submit. What would his fate be if he were cast out on his own, a stranger in the world? Was this the price to be paid for his future?

In the end, I said nothing and allowed it to happen.

After this, I hoped that Ishmael would be accepted and given his rightful place in the family, that he would be favored and trained to become the next patriarch. Instead, he was treated as a common servant, with even less kindness than before.

I went to Abraham, in a rage. "You made a promise to me and to my son."

"I have prayed for him," he said. "Yahweh has heard. Ishmael will be blessed. He will be the father of 12 princes. But he will not be the one to carry on the Covenant."

"Then the Covenant will die and be buried with you!" I shouted.

"No," he said. "Sarah is with child."

Strange how we can move through our daily routine even when hope is shattered. Like a detached observer, I watched life continue around me. Isaac was born. There was a great feast, with much rejoicing. I served the food and wine and heard them all praising God for the miraculous birth. Abraham took the infant in his arms and prayed.

"The promise of God is fulfilled," he proclaimed.

And everyone said, "Amen."

Now Sarah could no longer bear my presence. There were plenty of *other* servants and none of *them* reminded her of the painful past. One day she found Ishmael playing with little Isaac, tickling him, making him giggle, gently swinging him in the air. The sight of them, brothers together, ignited all the fear and guilt in Sarah's heart. She appealed to Abraham to cast us out—the contemptuous slave woman and her dangerous son. I did not expect that Abraham would show much concern for me, yet I still believed that he would not abandon his firstborn. I was mistaken.

Early the next morning, he came with a loaf of bread and a skin of water, led us out to the road, and pointed us toward the wilderness of Beersheba. I remember how he tried to smile and how it dissolved when he saw my face. We started walking. After a few steps I turned to look back. Abraham was gone.

The promise did not depend on Abraham alone, or Sarah, or Isaac, or on any one person, or any one people or nation. That's what I learned in the rest of my life. I found a wife for Ishmael in Egypt and became a grandmother many times over. My son became the powerful leader he was destined to be. And we worshiped the one God who is over us all.

Long after our separation, I heard a story about Abraham that changed my feelings toward him. It's said that he was tested by God, that he took young Isaac up on a mountain to sacrifice him to Yahweh. The story made me think of Sarah too. Did she know? Did she consent to it?

I imagined him standing with the knife poised above his son's small body, torn between vision and reality, balanced on that sharp blade edge where life places all of us sooner or later. Something held back his hand. Was it the voice of God booming from heaven? Or was it the voice of love shouting in his own soul? Can we tell the difference? *Is* there a difference?

When the news of Abraham's death came to us, Ishmael returned to help bury his father. By then, I was too old to make the journey, but I'm not sure I would have gone even if I had been able. I had already made my peace with Abraham and Sarah. They had wounded me, but they had been wounded themselves. We *all* need healing, and we all grope in our own ways after the one who can heal. They brought me to their God, and I met the God of us all.

Esau

Genesis 25–28, 32–33, 36

I AM ESAU, son of Isaac and Rebekah, Jacob's twin, but we were nothing alike—not in appearance, or temperament, or destiny. My brother was smooth, in more ways than one. He was fair (hah!). Fair-*skinned*, that is. I was the dark one, hairy, rough, blunt as a worn knife blade. Our struggle began in the womb. Being the elder, firstborn by moments, I was entitled, by custom and tribal law, to inherit my father's property and position, but that's not what happened. From birth—even *before* our birth, it seemed— Jacob was favored by Rebekah.

Strange, isn't it? What makes a certain child more pleasing to a parent's eye than another? What could I have done to be rejected before I could talk, before I could understand or influence my surroundings? Was I guilty of having the wrong complexion? Were my half-opened eyes set too close together, or too far apart? Did the shape of my infant face destroy some dream in a mother's heart? Did she hate me because of who I was, or did I become who I was because she hated me? I never found answers to these questions. For whatever reasons, Rebekah turned against me.

But *God* decided to balance this bitterness. My father Isaac had a particular fondness for *me*, especially as I grew to manhood. I was a hunter. I brought home fresh game that my father loved to eat and stories of the chase that he loved to hear. I think I touched his sense of adventure which he had to subdue in order to carry out his responsibilities as patriarch of the family. In me, he saw the strength and the boldness that had deserted him.

My brother Jacob was a farmer, planting seeds and harvesting crops. His risks had to do with waiting—waiting for sunshine, waiting for rain. He was domesticated. He stayed close to home, close to Rebekah.

Creeping up on the prey, racing after it until your heart feels about to burst, always in danger of being gored or clawed or bitten by some wild beast—it was not a life suited to my skinny, squeamish brother.

You've heard the story from his point of view, from *her* point of view, for it was Rebekah who shaped the details that were passed down to future generations. In that version, I appear as an ignorant, impetuous brute, driven by base instincts and crude passions. I am portrayed as stupid enough to sell my inheritance for a momentary satisfaction. The truth is a little more complicated.

Did I surrender my birthright for a taste of the soup that Jacob was preparing that day? It's true, I was hungry. The people who depended on me were hungry. We needed more than meat to live on. We needed vegetables and grains, the food that Jacob was cultivating in the fields around our home. If we pooled our resources, we might have been healthy and happy, *all* of us. We could have feasted together on the richness of the land, the plants that grew from the earth and the animals that walked on it.

But Jacob desired something more than a *solution* to our common problem. He wanted power. Power over me and my people. I asked for a piece of his land. He asked for my inheritance. It seemed reasonable at the time. After all, we were brothers. If either of us ran into difficulty with our bargain we would work it out not as strangers but as family. Peacefully. Lovingly. I misjudged my brother. Relinquishing my birthright may have been foolish, but I did not take it very seriously. Jacob did.

Besides, my careless oath, by itself, would not have been enough to reverse our fortunes. My father still intended the first share of his wealth to go to me. When he was old and bedridden, with his eyesight failing, he called me to his side. "Take your bow," he said. "Go out to the field and hunt for me. Let me taste savory meat one last time. And then I will bless you before I die."

As always, I hastened to do his bidding, noticing, as I left the tent, that Rebekah was standing close by, close enough to hear the instructions my father had given me. It was the opportunity she had been hoping for.

She went to Jacob and told him of her plan: Jacob would take my place. He would bring the meat to Isaac. He would receive the blessing.

Much as he wished to supplant me, I'm sure Jacob whined and pleaded in fear. "How can I pretend to be Esau? My father will not be tricked. He will recognize my voice. He will touch my hand and realize it is not rough and hairy like Esau's."

I can imagine Rebekah silencing his protests with a word.

"Enough! You will dress in Esau's clothes. You will have his smell. You will wrap your hands in goatskins. When your father asks who has come to his bedside, you will say, 'Esau.' And you will receive his blessing."

She ordered two lambs to be slaughtered and cooked them herself.

When I returned, much later, I found my father weaker than ever and confused. He surprised me by asking, "Who's there?"

"Esau," I said, and his face twisted in pain. It took few words for us to realize how the plot had been carried out. And we both knew that it could not be undone.

It was our belief that the words of a blessing or a curse, once spoken, could not be recalled. They formed a spirit apart from us, acting on its own, no longer under our control. It did not matter that Jacob had lied. He would now receive "the dew of heaven," grain and wine and the fatness of the earth. Peoples would serve *him* and nations would bow down to *him*!

I would have killed him if he had not fled to another country. His escape was disguised as a journey to seek a wife among our own people in Haran. He was sent to stay with Laban, Rebekah's brother.

I married also and moved my household to the country of Edom. Many years passed. I learned that my brother had grown rich in that time. My old wound had not healed.

The longing for home is a powerful force and, eventually, it led Jacob to give up safety and comfort in a foreign land and return to the danger of his birthplace, to face the brother he had wronged.

He sent messengers ahead. They were frightened to begin with. What I had to say frightened them even more. "Tell Jacob I am coming to meet him with four hundred men!"

Soon, there arrived a generous present from my brother—some of the best animals from his flocks. But even the finest gifts could not alter my memory or redeem the sins of the past. Was there *anything* that might redeem those sins? I asked myself: Was there a way to find peace, to trust each other, to be brothers once more? I could not be sure. I struggled with the thought, unaware, until later, that Jacob was wrestling with his own demon, or angel, on the other side of the Jabok River.

It was not an answer that came to me, but more of a feeling that came *over* me. I had wanted to release my pain in anger and violence. It was justified and I had the power to do it. But somehow I realized, beyond explanation, that rage would not free me from my suffering. I had wanted to punish my brother, but now I felt a greater power within me, the power to forgive. I had the ability to make peace, to give back to my brother a part of his life that was a part of my life too. Suddenly there was more joy in the thought of mercy than in the yearning for vengeance.

Still, I was not above putting a scare into him. I brought a small army with me and they looked ferocious enough to make even the strongest foe turn and run. But Jacob was not strong. He had filled out a little from years of the easy life with Laban, but he was not a fighter. He came forward alone, unarmed, head held high, ready to be cut down—which I'm sure he fully expected. He was, on that day, as brave as anyone I'd known.

His very defenselessness moved me deeply. His life was in my hands. How often I had prayed for this moment. God had answered but the outcome would be one that I never envisioned. I ran to him and threw my arms around him. He was stunned at first, unable to move, but then we were hugging and weeping together.

A small miracle in the grand scheme. It did not change the course of history. His people would eventually conquer my people. The prophecy came true. Edom did serve Israel. And the Covenant promise passed down through the sons of Jacob, not the sons of Esau. Jacob is the patriarch named with Abraham and Isaac. Esau is forgotten.

But on that day, on that spot by the Jabok River, we became brothers again, and I believe that our embrace can teach the world more than all the wars fought in our names. Vengeance is false comfort for our wounds. Only forgiveness can heal.

Leah

I AM LEAH, Jacob's first wife. Not first in order of preference. No, that would be Rachel, my younger sister. Jacob adored her. So did everyone else. So did I, as a child, living in her shadow, marveling at the power her beauty gave her, how she could manipulate those around her with the flash of a smile, a pout, or a wink. She was not cruel at heart, though she seldom looked deeply into her heart. She had simply learned to get her way by counting on the effect of her appearance. She would learn, later, that even the prettiest face cannot prevent disappointment. Even her lovely, sparkling eyes could shed bitter tears.

As the story has been told, Jacob traveled hundreds of miles to our country, in search of a wife. His mother, Rebekah, feared that he might marry a Canaanite or a Hittite, as his brother Esau had done. She pleaded with Isaac to send Jacob to Haran that he might choose a bride from among his kinsfolk. So he journeyed to the home of Laban, his uncle, to meet his cousins Leah and Rachel.

But stories are told in many ways and sometimes they are colored to hide disturbing facts. The truth is that Jacob was not seeking a wife. He was fleeing from his brother. He had tricked Esau out of his inheritance and his father's blessing, but the result of his plotting was not what he'd hoped for. He could not stay in the land he had deviously acquired. Esau, the hairy one, the brother he had wronged, sought to find him and kill him. Jacob, the schemer, had to escape into exile.

That is why he came to us without the accustomed dowry. That is why, when he extended his hand for marriage, it was empty. That is why he could only offer my father his services, in place of the gifts he could not present.

To Jacob, it was a reasonable bargain to satisfy his unreasonable passion. His unreasonable passion for Rachel. I know of this because, over the years, although she was the one he desired, breathlessly and unquestioningly, *I* was the one he confided in. I listened, too often, to the stories that broke my heart.

How they met. A romantic tale. A pastoral setting. The shepherds of my father's flocks, on a hill, by a well. The well covered by a large stone, requiring many hands to move it—so that no unscrupulous types could come along and take too much water for their own purposes.

Meeting the shepherds, Jacob inquired after Laban, and they pointed out his daughter, tending her father's sheep. His eyes fell upon Rachel—young, strong, and so very beautiful. She didn't notice him and so he saw her in her most natural, unaffected state, lifting her sweet face to the sunlight, breathing in the fragrance of the fields, relaxed, yet alert for the slightest whimper of the animals in her charge. He was captivated at once and forever.

Inspired by the sight of her, he found within himself a strength he never possessed before and single-handedly heaved the stone aside. He offered Rachel a cup of water, kissed her hand, and wept.

Love can turn anyone into a fool.

When my father heard of Jacob's arrival, he ran to meet him, embraced him, brought him home, and called for a celebration. Over the next month, Jacob trailed Rachel like a devoted pet, gaping at her with glazed, smitten eyes. Perhaps he would have asked for her hand sooner if the proposal were not against custom. As the elder daughter, I had the right to be given first in marriage. But my father also ignored tradition and agreed to the request. If Jacob would serve him seven years, Rachel would be his. I was not aware, then, of the plan that had entered my father's mind, a plan he would reveal to me only on the eve of the wedding day.

Jacob, to his credit, worked diligently during those years, increasing the flocks and the family income beyond all expectations. And he labored happily, with the goal of his efforts plainly in view whenever Rachel walked by. It pained me to see him stop and wipe the sweat from his forehead, smile at her, and then return to the work with fierce, joyous energy. For I had come to know him during that time, better, I'm sure, than my sister ever did. And, unfortunately for me, I had fallen in love with him.

We talked frequently. It's true, much of the time it was about Rachel. He was hungry for details about our childhood, the funny and sad experiences we shared. But his focus was always on her—what pleased her, what angered her, what frightened her, and what he could do to win her heart.

You see, the engagement seemed not to have touched my sister very profoundly. She accepted it with little emotion, enjoying Jacob's attention, but seemingly unchanged by the prospect of marriage. I doubt that she ever loved him.

Occasionally, my conversations with Jacob became more personal. He spoke of the weight of responsibility he bore as the heir of the vision. That's what he called it—the vision of his father and grandfather. The Covenant, the promise of Yahweh to our people. Faithfulness to this God above all gods would ensure our special place in the world. We would have a homeland. We would enjoy the fruits of the earth. We would have countless descendants to carry on the dream.

And then his expression would change and he would speak of

Esau with fear and remorse. "I am guilty of a terrible sin," he said, more than once. "I have gained an inheritance but I have lost a brother." His sorrow was real and it sliced through me too as I tried to comfort him. He sobbed uncontrollably. If he could have rewritten his past, I'm certain he would have done so without hesitation. If I could have removed his guilt and pain at the cost of my own life, I would have done so just as willingly.

But if there was affection between us, it never blossomed into love on Jacob's part. He valued my friendship, but anything more never occurred to him. He seemed even to assume that I understood this too—that because I was plain and, as everyone politely said, "weak-eyed," I could never *imagine* myself to be desired by such a great and handsome man as Jacob!

The "great men of the world" have much to learn about the true feelings of the rest of us!

I never thought of myself as ugly, just ordinary. Weak-eyed? Yes. A euphemism for my condition, which was near-total blindness. A progressive disease. Undetected in childhood, worsening in adolescence, full-blown in adulthood. As a little girl, I could see all the beautiful world around me. As a young woman, I could see well enough the difference between Rachel and myself. As an adult, I could see, barely, hazily, the face of the man I loved. Eventually, everything dissolved to formless gray.

At the end of the appointed period of service, the marriage was arranged. Among our people, the wedding feast lasts seven days. On the evening of the first day, the bride, with a veil covering her face, is led to the groom's tent and they are left alone to consummate their union.

The night before the opening banquet, as I worked with the other women preparing the food and drink, a servant approached and informed me that my father wished to speak with me.

He was unusually nervous as I stood before him and he avoided my eyes.

"Daughter," he began. "You know the ways of our people. It

is not right that you should be passed over for marriage because your younger sister has caught Jacob's eye. Love must adapt to law. Therefore, I have decided that tomorrow, when the celebrating is done and Jacob has gone to his bed, *you* will wear the veil, *you* will be the one to go in to your cousin."

"Father," I pleaded. "Not this way. He has not chosen me. I want him to *choose* me. Please. Don't deceive him. Don't humiliate me!"

He turned away to indicate the discussion was over.

"It is not a matter of choosing. Or deceiving. Am I not the head of my own family? It is not for you, or Jacob, to question. You will obey! And he . . . will accept my decision. In time, he will understand."

How strange to sit at the table, numb and blind, and listen to the revelry all around me—Rachel's high-pitched laugh, Jacob shouting above the music, his words coarse and wine-slurred, the commotion slowly settling to a low hum of voices. Being taken by the hand and guided toward my frightening appointment. Of all the sounds that night, the one I could never silence in my memory was the piercing cry of desolate pain that I recognized as the scream of my sister.

I don't know what I expected or what my father expected, but the morning after, when daylight revealed the lie, Jacob surprised us both. Suppressing his shock and anger, he left without a word and went directly to Laban. Calmly, he declared that though this marriage with Leah was based on falsehood, he would honor it nevertheless. He proposed to work an additional seven years to make Rachel his wife, but now *he* would dictate the terms of the arrangement. He listed his demands: equal authority over the family and in business matters, sharing the position and privileges of head of the tribe, and, when the time came for him to depart with his household, a generous portion of Laban's wealth. My father was in no position to argue.

I suppose our life together was not so different from that of most married people I knew. Love was hardly a requirement in those days. Happiness mattered little. What mattered was children. I was stupid enough to think that creating a child together would create love between us.

I gave birth to Reuben. Jacob was, if not overjoyed, at least relieved to have, at last, a male heir. Others followed: Simeon, Levi, Judah. But, even when he proudly gathered our sons in his arms, he spoke of Rachel, their approaching marriage, and the descendants *she* would bear for him.

After the long wait, he claimed her, but his hopes were not fulfilled. It seemed that Rachel was barren. Jacob blamed *her*, but I wondered if the fault were not his own. Often he had confessed to me of being intimidated by her "perfection," an attitude that seldom assists a man in the performance of his marital responsibility.

Rachel, in desperation, confronted him. "Give me children, or I will die."

It stung Jacob's pride, and he turned on her.

"Whose fault is this?" he shouted. "I am not withholding children from you. *God* is! I have *four* sons by Leah! Look to yourself to find the curse!"

His cruelty caused me to sympathize with my sister. Despite all that had set us in opposition, I realized that we shared the same struggle: how to live with or above or against the forces that controlled us. Choosing a path that offered some satisfaction and a bit of contentment was not easy for either of us.

I asked Reuben to gather mandrakes, a kind of fruit, something like plums, which we use to increase fertility. They were of little value to me since Jacob no longer came to my bed. I intended to present them to Rachel as a peace offering.

But she was as cold and ungrateful as ever. My emotions, bound up so tightly for so long, suddenly burst forth.

"Is there anything you do not feel entitled to? You have taken

my husband from me! I am married but I live alone, caring for
his children! Children he rarely bothers to speak to! You have his
love and it means nothing to you! What do you want?"

"I want the mandrakes," she said icily. "Give them to me, and
you can have your husband back. For one night!"

It shames me to say that I consented.

The mandrakes failed. It was not until several years later that
Rachel finally conceived. When Joseph was born, Jacob decided
to gather all his large family and return to his homeland. Wily as
ever, he convinced my father to reward him with only the speck-
led sheep and black lambs. Even so he went away with more than
half the flock. He left a rich man.

But wealth could not shield him, or any of us, from the difficult times ahead. Jacob still had to face Esau, who nursed the old
grievance and waited with his army in Canaan to take revenge on
his brother.

Joseph, idolized and pampered by his father, would one day
become a great leader, but Rachel did not live to see it. She would
die giving birth to her second son, Benjamin. Jacob would live
with sorrow for many years, believing that Joseph, his favorite,
had been killed.

And Leah? My role was less spectacular, yet no less important. Through me, as well as any patriarch, prophet, or king, the
promise was revealed. Though blind, I could *visualize* the truth:
that no imperfection of body or of character is unredeemable in
God's plan. The scorn of the world, the scars of this life, are not
the end of hope, but the beginning of faith.

Reuben

Genesis 37, 39–50

I AM REUBEN, firstborn of Jacob and Leah, the eldest of Jacob's twelve sons who sired the twelve tribes of Israel. I was no hero. I did not stride into the pages of history, marshaling events and witnesses to amplify my fame down through the generations. Most of my life was spent regretting one terrible sin of my youth.

In a critical moment, courage failed me. I stood silently by . . . no—let me confess it—I *took part* in the betrayal of my brother, Joseph. God knows the guilt I suffered and God alone could have redeemed it.

Joseph was the fifth son of Jacob, the *first* child of Rachel, the answer to her prayers; proof, after so many years, that she was not barren, as everyone had assumed. Coddled by his mother, spoiled by his father, Joseph grew to be an unpleasant, unlikable young man. His fine features, slender, graceful physique, and an air of disdain for the less favored caused his brothers, myself included, to hate him. To make matters worse, his pretension and sarcasm seemed to be condoned by my father.

The ultimate insult was delivered on his seventeenth birthday. Jacob presented him with a beautiful, expensive gift—the infamous "coat of many colors." Colorful, yes—nothing like the drab garments the rest of us wore to work in the pastures while Joseph

22

paraded his finery close to home. But the real affront cut much deeper. Unlike our ragged cloaks that exposed our strong, brown arms to the sun, Joseph's coat had *sleeves* that flowed to his wrists. A sign of indoor ease, privilege, nobility. A token of royalty!

The sniveling pest had the nerve to waltz out into the fields and model the new fashion for us! It did not surprise us to see him. He appeared regularly to spy on us and bring his tattletale reports back to Jacob. This time, noticing his unusual dress and a peculiar, self-satisfied glint in his eyes, we turned aside from the work and confronted him.

"Brothers," he said, smirking. "I have had a wonderful dream. In my dream, I am a bright star in the sky, the *brightest* star in the heavens. And in this dream, the sun, the moon, and eleven other stars are *bowing to me!*"

He laughed and walked away, the folds of his luxurious robe swirling around him.

"Worthless, lazy fool!" Simeon fumed.

"Yes," said Levi. "But a fool who has our father's ear, and his love, and maybe his wealth and power too, unless we do something."

"Do something?" I asked. "What can we do?"

Looking at their faces, I felt a chill run up my spine. A conspiracy began to take shape.

I listened to them argue over the details of their murderous plan and said little. My mind raced, searching for a way to prevent the crime without revealing the horror that seized me.

"No," I spoke, at last. "We must not shed his blood." I forced a smile. "Better to leave him in the hands of *nature's* justice. We dig a pit, too deep to climb out of, and tomorrow, when he arrives to taunt us again, he slips and falls into it. We're so busy at our work, we don't hear his screams for help. A few days later, we happen upon his poor, lifeless body."

Simeon picked up the thread.

"Or perhaps we find nothing more than his beautiful, blood-stained, birthday coat. O Father, what a tragedy. Our beloved brother mauled by some wild beast. Poor Joseph."

They settled on the plan—*my* plan—not realizing I had proposed it in the hope of saving my brother from death. If they left him in the pit, I could return to pull him out later. What explanation I might give my brothers for Joseph's survival I hadn't formulated. One problem at a time. If he lived, I would think of something.

Joseph unwittingly cooperated with the plot, coming out to the field the next day. We spied him at a distance.

"Here comes the dreamer," Levi said. "His dream is about to become a nightmare."

We surrounded him and watched his mocking expression melt into fear. We took hold of him. He began to whimper and beg for mercy. He struggled pathetically, but he was light as a feather as we pitched him into the trench.

Then my brothers sat down to eat their lunch and *enjoy* the desperate pleadings of their victim.

"See, we are all bowing to you now, Brother," Levi taunted him.

"Are you thirsty, Brother?" Simeon called and spilled a cup of water into the pit. "What kind of star is this? Must be a *falling* star! Not a *rising* star, otherwise he could ascend to the skies without our help!"

I left, went home, and waited for my brothers to return so that I could sneak back in darkness to save my brother. At the end of the day, they straggled in, their faces now somber and strained. The weight of the deed had settled in.

Simeon held the precious coat, torn and caked with dried blood. The blood was not Joseph's. It came from a goat they had slaughtered that day. Judah told the rest of the story.

A caravan of Ishmaelite traders had passed by that afternoon on their way to Egypt. It was not uncommon for such merchants to purchase strong, healthy young men and women on their journeys through our country and resell them in the city as slaves. For the price of twenty shekels, Joseph was sold into slavery, to sweat and suffer and die in a foreign land. A land we would never see. A *brother* we would never see again.

The news almost killed my father. He *wanted* to die, *begged* God to let him die. He put on sackcloth—the coarse, woolen girdle around the loins that signifies mourning. He grieved wildly, helplessly, for many months, and then quietly and deeply for years after. He kept the coat and held it tenderly in his hands as he wept night after night. We could not help hearing his cries of anguish and despair.

Time passed, and, if it did not heal the wound, as it is said to do, it forced us to concentrate on more immediate problems. Above all, food.

Twenty years later, famine had descended upon the land. Our sheep had nothing to graze on and we had nothing but the sheep to eat in order to survive. We could not hold out much longer.

We had heard that grain was still plenteous in only one place we could reach before dying on the road. In Egypt. Gathering all the riches that could be carried that far, Jacob sent his sons to the capital city of Memphis to buy food for our hungry people. Only Benjamin, the youngest, was left behind.

The journey was arduous. We lost nearly half of our company along the way. We would have turned back if this were not our last hope. Desperation gave us enough strength to reach the city.

In Egypt, we met with Pharaoh's minister of agriculture, a tall, dignified, stern official, who questioned us at length concerning our needs and our motives. With so many asking for aid in this crisis, the government needed to be cautious about its generosity. Egypt still had enemies and spies were everywhere, anxious to uncover some political advantage from an economic disaster.

"How do I know that *you* are not spies?" he asked.

"Excellency," I said. "We are twelve brothers, the sons of one man in the land of Canaan. We have no power to threaten your mighty nation. We have no secrets to conceal. We simply have no food."

At this, he moved aside and seemed to be struggling within himself.

"I have no reason to doubt you," he said finally. "Neither do I have sufficient evidence to trust you. Therefore, I shall keep only one in prison." He pointed to Simeon. "The rest of you will be given a modest amount of grain to take back to your people. But you must return here as soon as possible, and bring with you, as proof of your honesty, your brother Benjamin."

We turned our backs to the interpreter so that we could speak among ourselves without having the words translated.

"We have no alternative," I said.

"I am not afraid of his prison," Simeon boasted. "But Jacob will never send Benjamin! You know that!"

"Why must this be?" Judah whined. "Why are we treated as criminals when all we want is to feed our families?"

"Are we *not* criminals?" I shouted at him. "Do we not have the blood of our brother on our hands? I tried to warn you. You would not listen. This is the reckoning. For Joseph! For Joseph!"

The minister waved his hand impatiently and we fell silent. As we bowed in acceptance of his demands, I noticed tears in his eyes.

At first it appeared that Simeon had been right. Jacob remained adamant.

"I have lost Joseph!" he protested painfully. "And now Simeon! Shall I sacrifice Benjamin as well? No! He is the last remaining son of Rachel. I will not give him up. Tell me what evil spirit tempted you to reveal that one more brother had been left behind in Canaan?"

"Father," I said. "We were tricked! We fell into a *trap*! So many questions that seemed innocent, routine: How many people must be fed? What kind of supplies are most needed? Is your father alive? Are there any more brothers at home? How could we know he would demand to see Benjamin? But if we were stupid, it doesn't matter now. We have brought back only enough grain to last a month, at most. We cannot survive unless we go back, unless we go back *with Benjamin*. I have only my life to offer in place of his—my life and the life of my two sons. Father, I make this vow, in Yahweh's name: slay my own children if I fail to bring back Benjamin alive and unharmed!"

The next morning, Jacob gave his answer.

"If it must be so—and only God knows why it must be—take gifts with you: balm and honey, almonds and myrrh, and gold . . . and Benjamin. God grant you mercy before the rulers of Egypt. I am bereaved of my children. I am bereaved."

In Egypt, a feast awaited us, presided over by the same official we had met on our previous visit. He had ordered that Benjamin be seated beside him at the table. In the midst of the festivities, he rose and asked Benjamin to stand at his side. Then, he embraced him and said, with great emotion, "God bless you, my son."

He dismissed everyone from the room except for us and spent a long time studying each of our faces.

"Look at *my* face," he said quietly. "Do you not know me?"

As if through the sudden clearing of a mist, I recognized him. He saw it in my eyes.

"Yes, Reuben, I am . . . Joseph. Brothers, don't be afraid. I am not a ghost. Come, let me embrace you."

"Forgive us," Simeon pleaded through his tears.

"I *have* forgiven you," Joseph said. "Although you meant me harm, God brought good out of evil, brought me here—to power—in order to preserve life. But, be warned, the crisis is not past. The famine has lasted two years. There are still five years more in which there will be no plowing, no harvest. Pharaoh has given permission for you to settle here among us. I will give you wagons to take back to Canaan that you may bring your wives and children to this land. Bring nothing else for it will not be needed. The best of all Egypt will be available to you. And bring your father . . . *my* father, that I may see him again."

The shock was almost too great for Jacob to bear. The precious son he had lost had come back to life. And now he was asked to move his entire household to another country. But the hope of seeing Joseph once more overpowered all other considerations.

We traveled to Egypt, and settled in the land of Goshen. On Joseph's authority, we were given the job of herding the Pharaoh's cattle there. The years of famine continued, as Joseph had predicted; but we survived, even prospered. Eventually, we became more accustomed to life in our new homeland.

When my father died, we carried him back to Canaan and buried him there, according to his request.

We were rich by then. But our descendants would not fare so well in Egypt.

Still, the truth that so dramatically changed our lives, we passed on to our children. Adversity can lead to redemption. In grief or guilt, in poverty, hunger, or slavery, whether or not we see it or know it or understand it, God is always working to save us.

Zipporah

Exodus 2-4, 18

I AM ZIPPORAH, the wife of Moses, the great law giver, hero and liberator of the Hebrew people. My husband was not easy to understand or to live with. Called by God to a position of power high above the dull drudgery of common folk, he had responsibility for *hundreds* of families, not merely his own. I was part of his entourage, his larger following.

He came to Midian, my homeland, as a fugitive, a criminal. He had been an important official in the Egyptian government, but, one day, he had come upon an overseer abusing a Hebrew slave. He drew his sword and killed the guard.

Pure compassion for the oppressed? A little more complicated than that. A little more *personal* than that. Moses had learned, shortly before this incident that he himself was a Hebrew! Adopted as an infant by a daughter of the Pharaoh, raised as a member of the noble class. Now, he realized that, by birth, *he* was of the race that toiled in the mud, piling up bricks and mortar, raising grandiose monuments to the glory of the Pharaoh. Now he wanted to know all about these people, *his* people.

After the murder, he had to flee. He came to Midian not just for safety but also because his secret inquiries concerning the

Hebrews had revealed that God, Yahweh, was still worshiped here. The slaves in Egypt, after three hundred years, scarcely remembered the God of their ancestors. In Midian, Moses would search for a link to his religious heritage.

On the day he arrived, we had come to the well to water the flocks. As often happened, rival shepherds were there—big, burly brutes who enjoyed taunting a woman who dared to do "a man's work." When they'd had enough fun, they turned serious and menacing and tried to drive us off. Moses stepped forward, outnumbered, but impressive. We were moments away from terrible violence. But the bullies backed down and moved on, bragging about what they *could* have done *if* they had chosen to fight.

From that day on, whatever the problems between us, I never questioned my husband's courage.

He drew water for the animals and for me, accompanied me home, and stayed with us. Over the next months, he developed a close bond with Jethro, my father, who taught him about our God. Yahweh lived on the holy mountain and was stronger than the other gods of the earth—a frightening, angry God who demanded worship and sacrifice but offered little practical help to our people.

Moses had his own ideas about this God. He debated, even contradicted, my father. He described Yahweh as the *supreme* power, the one and only one who controlled *all*, who might appear at the top of a mountain, but could be present anywhere, who could hear and be *moved* by the groaning of the people, who would intervene and scatter our enemies and free us from bondage.

Strangely, the Yahweh Moses described terrified me more than the one I had known before. If God could be *everywhere*, watching us *always*, and if God *cared* about our lives, surely much more would be expected of us than the tedious rituals we performed. Such a god would require a response from our hearts.

Of course, I was not invited to participate in these weighty discussions. In fact, Moses seemed hardly to notice me at all. Then, one day, without a word of warning, he entreated my father for my hand in marriage. As I was the oldest of seven daughters, it was an acceptable proposal. My father smiled on the arrangement.

What motivated this once great prince of Egypt to wed a simple, country shepherd? Certainly love and desire had not arisen between us, and, honestly, such feelings *never* came to be in all the years that followed. I believe he decided the union would fit his grander plans—somehow confirming the bond with his people and his God.

I dutifully bore him two sons: Gershom and Eliezar, and for a while we settled into a reasonably normal life in Midian, although I was aware of my husband's restless spirit. He had produced a family, but he had not found a home. Gershom, the name he chose for our first child, means "I have sojourned in a foreign land."

The upheaval began when news reached us that the Pharaoh had died. A few days later, Moses came home from tending the flocks and announced that he had received a vision. In the wilderness, a bush that burned but was not burnt. Removing his shoes, kneeling upon holy ground, he had heard a voice: "I am the God of Abraham, the God of Isaac, the God of Jacob . . . the God of Moses. I am Yahweh. I Am Who I Am. I Am Who I Will Be."

Yahweh had heard the cries of the enslaved Hebrews. Yahweh would bring them up out of their affliction in Egypt and lead them to a land of milk and honey. And Moses would be God's instrument. The humble shepherd's staff in his hand would become the rod of divine power.

Moses had no need for *my* consent, but he did seek the approval of my father, who, enthralled by the miraculous account, released Moses with a blessing: "Go in peace."

Peace was the last thing we found on our wandering journey!

We were set upon donkeys and led out into the wilderness—me with Eliezar in my arms, Moses on foot before us, gripping the rod of Yahweh which pointed the way to Egypt.

To Egypt! To the Pharaoh! Can you imagine the absurdity of this mission?

"Let my people go!"

To the ruler of the world! Listen, King of Egypt, to this tiny bug in your vast realm! "Let my people go!"

"*Your* people, Moses?" I could hear the Pharaoh respond with amusement and sarcasm. "Do you mean *my* slaves, whose *fate*, whose *extra* punishment or *brief* respite, whose every breath *I* control? Let *them* go? Let them *go*? Or else? Or else *what*? Or *else* an impostor-criminal-suddenly-sanctified prophet will bring down the wrath of his puny, local god upon my entire nation? I am terrified. *Please*, spare us, O mighty deliverer!"

At our first stop along the way, our "mighty deliverer" became deathly ill and I became alarmed. Perhaps I had misjudged the power of his convictions, the power of his God. As I dabbed his feverish skin with cold water, he whispered, hoarsely: "The sign . . . the sign of the Covenant. . . . We have disobeyed . . ."

I understood. Circumcision—a practice rejected by my family ages ago. I had refused to allow my sons to be so mutilated. But now it seemed undeniable, God was angered by my stubbornness. I decided that temporary suffering was preferable to infinite condemnation.

I chose Eliezar, because he was younger and less likely to recall the pain when he had grown to manhood. I spent many hours sharpening a jagged stone for the terrible task. Before carrying out the hideous deed, I could not resist standing over my husband, sick as he was, and pouring out my rage: "You are a bridegroom of blood to me!"

But the very next morning, Moses improved. A few days later

he was almost fully recovered. In a week, he was back at the head of our caravan, leading us on to a destination he alone envisioned. I wondered, then, if I would ever understand him, or his God.

In Egypt, there were more surprises. When the plagues came, Pharaoh *was* terrified, though he resisted until death visited the firstborn son of every family in the land. Except for the slaves. According to plan, that avenging angel passed over every Hebrew home. A miracle! An act of God! Against all logic. Reality forced me to *question* logic. Experience is its own explanation.

In my life, I witnessed the improbable, the impossible, day after day. A mighty sea split down the middle, forming a pathway for the chosen and a deadly trap for their pursuers. Water from dry rock. Food for the starved floating down gently from heaven into our hands. I have nothing more, nothing better, than my own life to tell me that God knows us and cares for us.

Once in many ages, a Moses is born, is snatched from the current of destruction, and is raised up to become the holy voice of freedom. But the rest of us—striving and struggling, fragile yet hopeful, determined but awed by a universe that absorbs our little lives and remains unchanged by our passing dreams—*we* are the reason that God comes, in a pillar of fire or a whisper of inspiration, to conquer injustice, to deny despair, to save us. If the Yahweh I have learned to trust cares about the great events of history, that wondrous God must also care about the misery we go through to reach our own hearts and the hearts of others. And our most private, unspoken needs must be *not* so different from the needs of the world this God longs to see, the world this God will surely, ultimately, cause to be.

Gideon

I AM GIDEON, a farmer who became a warrior and a judge of Israel. A hundred years before my birth, Joshua had led our people out of the desert into the land of Canaan, our "promised land." But if God had promised this land to *us*, the people living here did not see it that way. To them, we were invaders, and, truthfully, it is hard to argue otherwise. And yet, our competing claims were so ancient, our histories so intertwined, it would have been nearly impossible to establish a clear, unassailable right to ownership of that land. We were racial and cultural kinsfolk, but oftentimes the possibility of compromise is least likely within the family.

The terrible warfare that began in those times continued down to my own day. My people had become entrenched in the central hill country, but we could not dislodge the Canaanites from the plains and coastal areas. We lived with the constant threat of attack: the Philistines pressing inland from the sea, the Moabites and Amonites from the other side of the Jordan, and the Midianites—our worst enemy—charging out of the Arabian desert.

We were not well organized or well equipped to respond to the danger. The twelve tribes were scattered and only loosely united, chiefly by our common religion. We gathered annually for worship at Shiloh where the ark of the covenant was housed. But we had no central government, no capital city, no permanent army. Each tribe raised its own militia and usually fought its own battles. In military emergencies, an extraordinary leader might step forward to assemble us under one banner. More often, we handled our separate affairs separately.

It was an age of transition: a nomadic people slowly adjusting to a more settled existence. Even in Canaan, many chose to live in their familiar tents while others built simple houses out of stone. We learned the art of construction from some of our less-hostile neighbors. And much more too: methods of farming, how to make pottery and furniture. In time, we began to intermingle, even intermarry, with the local population. But such intimate contact involved risks—risks, above all, to our faith. Canaanites and Israelites believed in different gods. Tolerance too easily led to compromise.

My own father, Joash, had built an altar to Baal and revered Asherah, the sacred tree of Astarte, the goddess of fertility. He had forgotten Yahweh's commandment: "You shall worship no other God but me."

The work of farming was backbreaking and precarious, regulated by the seasons but subject to the whims of nature. We harvested olives in early autumn and soon after planted wheat and barley to be reaped in the spring when the winter rains relented. In summer, we picked fruits and vegetables and grapes for wine. But we faced drought, locusts, and a fierce, dry wind—another enemy from the desert—that robbed moisture from the air and withered the crops.

Far more destructive than the elements were the Midianites. For seven years we had endured their brutal raids. Their favorite prey was my own small tribe of Manasseh. In the village of Ophrah, where I lived, the fear was constant, resistance impossible. The Midianites had tamed the camel for use in battle. To see these clumsy but surprisingly swift creatures descending upon the town brought terror to our hearts. Many of our people fled to caves in the surrounding hillsides and remained there year round, like timid little animals.

The pattern had been established. The Israelites sowed and the Midianites reaped. At times, after driving us off, they would literally encamp in our fields for days or weeks—however long it took to collect and consume the fruits of our labor.

I prayed, relentlessly, for Yahweh to deliver us. And then, one day, the answer came, but it was hardly what I expected or desired.

I was grinding wheat, not as I should have been doing, upon the threshing floor, but secretly, in a wine press, so as not to alert our enemies. Suddenly, I was overcome with shame and anger.

"Why, Yahweh?" I called out defiantly. "If you are the true, almighty God, why do you allow your people to suffer so? Where are your great, liberating deeds, recounted of old? Did the miracle of the Exodus exhaust your power? Have you abandoned us to the evil of the world? Who will save us?"

Then, I heard a voice. Not my own, but within me. *"You will save the people, Gideon. My power will be with you."*

I fell to me knees.

"Yahweh," I whispered. "How can *I* do your will? My clan is the weakest in Manasseh, and I am the least in my family."

Again, I heard it. *"My power will be with you."*

I had no idea how to save my people, but knew that to accomplish anything, I must first turn my people back to our God. We could not trust in Yahweh's protection as long as we gave part of our allegiance to other gods. During the night, I destroyed that altar to Baal and chopped down the tree of Asherah.

The next morning, the townspeople were frightened and furious. Bad enough to be at the mercy of the Midianite bullies, but now I had insulted a deity who might defend us.

Ironically, my father, bless him, came to my defense. "Consider the truth!" he challenged them. "Can a mortal overrule a god? If Baal *is* a god, let him contend for himself . . ."

The rebellious mob backed down. On the very spot of the sacrilege we built an altar to Yahweh.

The danger increased. The Midianites had crossed the Jordan and were encamped nearby in the Valley of Jezreel.

I sent word to the tribes, particularly the northern tribes, Asher, Zebulun, and Naphtali. They responded quickly. In a week, we had assembled an army of thousands. But it was a crude force—most of the recruits untrained, undisciplined, some no more than innocent, smooth-faced boys. Another plan would have to be devised. I handpicked three hundred of the strongest-looking men and dismissed the rest. Still, I had no design for the operation. An uninformed leader following the divine injunction. I needed more information and I had to get it firsthand.

In the darkness of a stormy night, I infiltrated enemy lines. Sneaking up to the outskirts of their camp, I could see the soldiers and the camels asleep. A sudden rustling close by froze me. Two Midianite guards sprawled on the hill just below me. One snored loudly, but the other was speaking to his dozing comrade or to himself.

"This battle will not be so easily won. I've heard the Israelites have a new general, someone named Gideon, who's put together an army. Of course, they'll be no match for us, but even so, this time some of us might get killed. You know, our soldiers aren't used to casualties."

I had found the missing piece to my battle plan. If this rumor had circulated among the Midianite soldiers, I could capitalize on it. If they feared engagement with an unexpectedly formidable army, we would confirm their fears.

Trumpets, torches, and huge, empty stone jars—these were

the props I needed to play out the scene. I instructed my men to take up positions encircling the Midianite camp. At a signal from me, they were to blow the trumpets, raise the torches, smash the jars, and yell for all they were worth, "A sword for Yahweh and for Gideon!"

The noise that shattered the peaceful night terrorized our already nervous enemies. They leaped, half-naked, from their beds, in panic and confusion, scrambled up the hills and into our swords. Some turned and fled toward the Jordan, but there they met another army—soldiers of the tribe of Ephraim whom I had ordered to stand at the shore of the river to cut off the escape route.

The Midianites were routed. Their power over us was broken.

The victory brought some security for a while. We had defeated a mighty enemy. But we had *many* enemies. I wish I could say this was the last war our people fought.

In my life, I witnessed much bloodshed that was considered necessary and called righteousness in the name of God. But the older I got, the more I doubted that God had planned these contests of death. The jealousy, hatred, and stupidity that cause them must surely be flaws of the *creatures*, not the *Creator*!

I am remembered as a hero, but anyone who has seen war, as I have, knows that there is little honor to be found in it and little hope to be gained by it. Peace, understanding, love . . . if there is a promised land, that's what it is. And that's how we'll get there.

Naomi

Ruth 1–4

I AM NAOMI, wife and widow of Elimelech of Bethlehem. My name means "joy," but my life was filled with great sorrow. Who would have thought my story would have a happy ending?

In my time the Hebrew tribes had settled down to a reasonably comfortable life in the land of Canaan, though the hostility of the neighboring peoples kept us apprehensive and vigilant. Even minor disputes could lead to war.

In Bethlehem, we farmed a rough, stony plateau, an area west of the Dead Sea, growing wheat, barley, and grapes, pruning olive and fig trees. But our industry depended upon fickle weather, erratic rainfall. Drought and flooding posed alternating threats. Famine was not uncommon. We had braved several disasters over the years, but when nature turned on us once again, my husband decided it was time to migrate in search of more fertile ground. We packed up our possessions and with our two sons, Mahlon and Chilion, departed for Moab.

Our destination was no more than fifty miles from Bethlehem, but, to me, it seemed like another world. The Moabites shared our ancestry and spoke a dialect similar to our own, but we were aliens, intruders in their eyes. In turn, my people regarded the

Moabites as uncivilized pagans. They worshiped a god called Chemosh who delighted in the sacrifice of children—babies thrown into a blazing furnace! *Our* law condemned such crimes: "You shall not give any of your children to the fire . . ."

Not all the Moabites were so barbaric. Elimelech had conducted business and even developed friendships with some of the more enlightened ones. Now they offered us assistance upon our arrival, made it possible for us to purchase farmland and a modest home. We would never be rich, but at least now we put food on the table. My husband worked hard. I cared for our little boys. We were sure our situation could only improve.

Elimelech was a vigorous man, hard-muscled and brown-skinned from long hours under the sun. I had not once seen him ill in all our years together. But one day in the fields, he dropped his cutting tool, fell down among the rows of wheat, and died.

At first, I was simply numb, my heart sealed like a tomb, afraid to feel, afraid to face the consequences of his death. Even as we laid him in the grave, as I spoke a short prayer over him, I could not cry. Finally, alone in our bed that night, a flood of grief and pain and fear swept over me. "How can this be?" I sobbed. "What will happen to us now?"

But by next morning, looking into the faces of my frightened sons, I resolved that no misfortune, no affliction, no obstacle would keep me from providing for my family.

I did as much as I could myself and hired day laborers for the rest. As my sons grew into strapping young men, they took on the greater part of the work. Over the years, we got by.

At age eighteen Chilion came to me with surprising news. He intended to marry—a Moabite girl named Orpah. Somehow I had always assumed we would one day return to our homeland and my sons would find their brides among our own people. Chilion dismissed my hope as a silly dream. He was impatient.

"We are here to stay," he said. "I am a man now. It's time for me to have a family, to make my home, and I will do it in this land!"

My misgivings soon disappeared. Orpah was a shy, gentle girl whose presence in the house eased my own burdens. I was getting older and appreciated another set of hands to help with the chores.

When Mahlon announced that he too had chosen a Moabite for his wife, I was prepared to welcome her as a daughter. I could not know then what a faithful daughter she would become. Ruth, with her shining eyes and beautiful smile, with her kindness and inner strength, restored joy to my life.

I counted myself blessed—with a happy family and the prospect of grandchildren one day, with crops ripening outside our door and sweet wine to drink with our evening meal. A good life, even if it had to be in Moab.

But what was it about this land that brought death?

The sickness seized Mahlon first. He burned with fever for six days. Ruth and I mixed herbs and roots, brewed them into a tea or rubbed them into his flushed skin, but nothing helped. Then, Orpah collapsed and we had to put her to bed, weak and shivering. My own face was warm to my touch but I decided to ignore it. Finally, Chilion was stricken and the disease, as if gathering strength, attacked him more ferociously than the others. Only Ruth escaped infection and she ran from bed to bed with blankets and cold water. When I could no longer stand, I sat in a chair and prayed.

After two days of agony, Chilion ceased his struggle. I held his cold, still body in my arms. That same night, Mahlon died.

Orpah recovered. My fever stayed mild and eventually faded. Ruth nursed us until we were out of danger.

The grief was unimaginable, constant, paralyzing. And, in the midst of it all, we were forced to make decisions about our future, for now we were in danger of becoming homeless.

Women could not inherit property. At best, a female "heir" might deed an estate to her closest male relative. Orpah and Ruth had fathers and brothers who might help them salvage some of the land and their possessions, but I was alone. They could return to their families and, in time, find new husbands. I was a foreigner, poor, past the age for childbearing—what man would pick me for a wife?

I had one choice open to me . . . to go home!

I loved Ruth and Orpah as daughters and couldn't bear the thought of saying goodbye. I delayed telling them of my decision as long as I could, but when my few belongings were packed, I had to face them. Expecting them to try to persuade me to stay, I was surprised when they insisted on going with me!

"No," I said. "It is too much to ask. I will not ask it of you. You will be strangers in my land. I have no means to support you. Here, at least, you can return to your old life and, in time, start a new one. What will you do in Bethlehem?"

Orpah lowered her eyes in sad, silent acceptance, but Ruth protested.

"In Bethlehem I will be with *you*! Do not ask me to abandon you, Mother. Where you go, I will go. Your people will be my people, your God my God. Where you live, I will live."

How could I argue against such selfless love or reject so pure a gift, though I felt unworthy of it? After a tearful parting with Orpah, Ruth and I headed into the desert toward our uncertain future.

Rumors had reached us of the lifting of the famine in Judah. When we came to the green hills at the edge of my village and looked down on fields of ripe wheat, our hopes were confirmed. The spring harvest had just begun and would last another seven weeks—a blessed opportunity for the poor to collect the scraps left behind by the workers in the fields. Now, as one of the poor myself, I had to admit I was grateful for this chance to simply survive. But I was too old to do the gleaning. I had to depend on Ruth.

At harvest time, young men, and some women too, passed through the rows of grain, swinging their sickles, slicing the stalks. Bunches of barley or wheat were then bound into sheaves and set aside to be ground into flour or meal. But some of the stalks were missed or dropped, and these could be gathered by the gleaners.

For Ruth, the work would be more than hard. It might also be dangerous. The men would not necessarily be pleased by the presence of a stranger, a foreigner. Or, perhaps, because of her beauty, they might be entirely *too* pleased. But we had no alternative. Ruth joined the other scavengers.

At the end of the first day, she told me of a tall, handsome man who appeared to be supervising the harvest. He noticed her and asked one of the laborers about her.

"A Moabite," the man answered. "I've never seen her before."

The distinguished overseer approached Ruth and lifted her from her knees.

"I am the *owner* of this land," he said. "My name is Boaz."

"Boaz!" I interrupted Ruth's story, my heart leaping. "I *know* him! A *kinsman* of my husband! What did you say to him?"

She had given him her name and a brief account of our plight, and he had responded compassionately! Dear God, here was a source of salvation!

He instructed her to continue gleaning within the borders of his property, to stay close to the other women under his protection. He warned his men to keep a respectful distance from her and to make sure she had water when she was thirsty.

Ruth dared to ask, "Why have I found favor in your sight, sir?"

Boaz replied: "You have been faithful to the mother of your husband—more faithful than *I* have been. Now, I will carry out my responsibility."

Ruth repeated his words to me without understanding their significance, but *I* understood.

"It is our law," I explained. "Levirate marriage. If a husband dies and leaves no son behind, the wife becomes the responsibility of his closest male relative. He must become her protector. I am too old for marriage, but all is not lost. Tomorrow, you will bathe and anoint yourself with fragrant oils, put on your best clothes, and go to the threshing floor. Say nothing, only be sure you are noticed by Boaz. At the end of the day, when he has finished eating and drinking, observe which tent he enters to sleep. Go to him, uncover his feet, and lie there. He will recognize the sign. He will know what to do."

No doubt Boaz, a middle-aged man by then, was flattered by the attention of a lovely young girl, but he was influenced not by lust but by principle. His duty and his desire would have led him to propose to Ruth, but he knew of another, closer kinsman whose rights preceded his own. He could not marry Ruth unless custom were satisfied.

The next morning, he went to the gate of the city. Here the merchants set up shops, townsfolk gathered to gossip, and the elders of Bethlehem met to settle disputes among the people— from controversies about property lines and poaching of livestock to more intricate questions of religious requirements. Ten men were needed for a quorum. On this day, more than enough were on hand to judge the case. The kinsman with first claim to Ruth had also been summoned.

With my fate in the balance, I could not resist the temptation to spy on their deliberations. I stood as close as I dared to their circle, pretending to bargain with one of the tradesmen, and listened intently.

Boaz spoke: "Naomi, the widow of Elimelech, has returned from Moab. Her sons died in that land and now she is alone, except for a daughter-in-law named Ruth. As a relative of

Elimelech, I am prepared to obey the law of levirate marriage, but there is one here whose privilege comes before mine, and I defer to him."

The man, sitting across from Boaz, stroked his beard thoughtfully.

"I am grateful for your consideration," he said. "Boaz, as we know well, is always honorable. But I have a wife and family and a small farm that I have tended since my youth. It is little enough inheritance for my sons. If I marry again and produce more sons, my tiny piece of land will have to be divided even further. I must think of the family I *have*, not of a family I *might* have. Boaz, if you are willing, take my right of redemption yourself."

With that, the man removed his sandal and handed it to Boaz who held it up for the elders to witness—a symbolic gesture. The contract had been sealed. It would bring blessing upon us all.

Ruth was to have the happiness she greatly deserved, and it would bring me a new happiness as well. She married Boaz, and bore him a son named Obed. Holding the infant in my arms, I realized that of all the dreams I'd ever had, the *best* one had come true. I didn't know, didn't need to know, that Obed would be the father of Jesse and Jesse would be the father of David, the king. More than sufficient was the joy of raising my grandson, seeing him take his first steps, teaching him all I knew about this perplexing world we live in and standing back to watch him miraculously become a whole, separate, striving, vulnerable, beautiful person!

We put so many restrictions on our love. I learned much from Ruth who loved so freely. We worry about differences of race, of color, of custom, of language, of religion. God, I believe, is not so worried. God knows what's best in *all* of us and it's not so different in *any* of us. And the future, often so blurry and frightening to us, is always clear in the eyes of God.

Jonathan

1 Samuel 15–20

I AM JONATHAN, the son of one king, the beloved friend of another, forced to choose between them. Blessed or cursed—I cannot be sure—with an honesty seldom valued by the powerful, reluctantly entangled in political intrigue, I became an instrument of God to redirect the history of Israel by simply trusting my conscience, by following my heart.

Saul, my father, assumed the throne in difficult days. Israel was not a nation then, but a loose affiliation of independent tribes dispersed through the land. We had enemies on all sides, the most formidable being the Philistines who swept down upon Canaan with a great army and superior weapons, capturing land, taking slaves, terrorizing our people.

If we had a leader, recognized by the tribes, it was Samuel, the last of the judges. Not a *ruler*, strictly speaking. *A prophet*, respected for his spiritual guidance, but limited in authority over public policy. The heads of the clans felt free to contradict his wisdom when it conflicted with more practical views.

As they did when they came to him clamoring for a king to unite and protect them. The prophet argued: "*Yahweh* is our King, the *only* King!"

The leaders of the delegation insisted. "We can learn from our neighbors, even from our enemies! We must imitate their success! We need one, strong voice to call us out of bondage. We need a king, like the other nations!"

How ironic! Israel's strength had always been built on the willingness, the *determination*, to be *un*like other nations!

But the tide had turned, and it rushed too swiftly for Samuel to stand against it. The people of the promise demanded to have their first earthly king . . . King Saul, my father.

He fit the description: tall, handsome, arrogant. As I knew from my own experience, he was also unpredictable, as changeable as our weather, at one moment a warm ray of sunlight, at another a sudden clap of thunder.

Both Samuel and Saul had their own, distinct misgivings. Even when the tribal elders were summoned to Mizpah to affirm his kingship, my father hesitated to appear before the crowd and accept the heavy responsibility for their welfare. It was a burden too great for the strength of any one man, and my father's strength was not always . . . dependable. Still, in the end, he bowed to their will.

But kingship remained a perplexing concept—to the ruler and the ruled. Organized government—a questionable novelty. Saul had no complete command over the tribes. We had no set-up for civil service, no taxes, no effective court system, no grand palace to inspire the awe of the citizenry. In fact, during the early years of his reign, my father continued to plant his crops, continued to see himself as a farmer, temporarily exalted to royal status.

As king, my father did quickly address our most serious need: security. He trained a sizable army and deployed several regiments in the countryside around Bethel to repel further attacks by the Philistines. I, myself, having reached manhood and straining to make my mark on the world, was given command of a thousand experienced soldiers to protect our capital. And *I* delivered the first blow to the enemy—a surprise mission against the Philistine garrison at Geba. The satisfaction of victory was short-lived, praised by the people but rightly criticized by my father. I had provoked a retaliation I never imagined. The Philistines soon returned in force.

We massed our army at Gilgal to meet them, but when we saw the thousands of Philistine chariots, horsemen, archers, and footsoldiers spreading out across the valley, our courage vanished. My father had pledged to wait for Samuel to offer the sacrifice necessary before battle, but after seven tense days, the prophet had not arrived. Our recruits began to desert, a few at first, and then in large numbers. Our entire force dwindled to no more than six hundred men.

In desperation, Saul decided to perform the ritual himself. Never very religious, my father mumbled some prayers and shouted orders to the troops to take up their positions for the encounter. In the midst of the scurrying that ensued, Samuel appeared, powerful, righteous, furious.

"Do you not trust your God?" he shouted. "Will *you* stand in the place of God's prophet, Saul? Is your oath meaningless? Are *you* a king above Yahweh?"

I'm sure my father would have dropped to his knees and begged forgiveness, but at that moment trumpets sounded and the battle began. The instincts of a general took over.

We would have been decimated that day, if not for circumstances unforeseen by the enemy, or by us. In the heat of the conflict, Israelite mercenaries who had joined our oppressors suddenly turned on the Philistine soldiers beside them. Seeing this, the deserters from our army, who had fled to the surrounding hills, returned to fight. The Philistines were routed, their occupation forces pushed back, our territory regained.

But my father's religious blunder haunted him and he lived in fear that Samuel's dire prediction would come true. "Now, your kingdom shall not continue . . ."

Tormented, melancholy, suspicious, issuing rash, cruel judgments, prone to erratic behavior, Saul became a cause for concern among his advisors. To soothe his rage, they brought to court a young man from Bethlehem who was said to play the lyre so sweetly that the sound could calm the most ferocious animal. His name was David and he proved to be as charming as his music. My father adored him. So did we all.

He had the voice of an angel. It flowed like a gentle stream, clear and unwavering, soaring to the highest notes effortlessly, then floating softly down to a rich bass tone. He composed whole songs on the spot from the suggestions of his audience. Instinctively, he chose words that raced to our hearts and filled our eyes with tears.

David was as beautiful as anyone I had ever seen. Tall and graceful, with sharply sculptured features, softened by his fair skin and warm brown eyes. When he smiled, it was like the flaring of a hundred candles.

Our friendship did not get off to a good start. Intimidated by his poise, his talent, his unaffected manner, I treated him with the scorn I considered appropriate for a mere servant. When I was at my worst, prancing about with hypocritical disdain, David would smile—lighting those candles again—and say, "Jonathan, the world recognizes that you are above me in station, but our hearts refuse to accept it." Gradually, I let down my guard and spoke to him as I had never imagined speaking to anyone before. I confessed that at the very center of my being I could find no desire to be a king.

"Yes," he said. "Being king is a heavy burden. But I will bear it gladly."

I laughed. A singing shepherd on the throne of Israel!

"It *will* be," he said. "I have been chosen."

Once again, the Philistines had marched into Judah. Saul led our army out to meet them.

The two camps were no more than half a mile apart. We could see their archers crouched with bows in hand, swordsmen in formation, the sun glinting off their unsheathed weapons, and messengers running between the battalions with last-minute orders.

And then, one of their soldiers moved forward and began to walk toward us, alone. With each step, he seemed to grow larger, and we realized, in a matter of moments, this was no illusion. He was twice the size of a normal man, in a bronze helmet and a massive coat of mail, armed only with a javelin that looked tiny beside his huge body.

When he was close enough to be heard, he called out in a rumbling voice, "I am Goliath, champion of the Philistines. Undefeated in combat with any man, or many men. Find among you a hero to face me. If he can conquer Goliath, the army behind me will withdraw and you may return safely to your homes. But if I kill him, as I intend—when I crush his bones in my bare hands— you will surrender and bow down to your new masters!"

A frightening silence was followed by an unexpected, confident cry.

"I am not a hero! Only a shepherd!"

I recognized David's voice and watched him push his way to the front of our battle line. He carried a sling and now he stooped to pick several stones from the ground, continuing to speak.

"Only a shepherd, but a shepherd knows how to take care of ugly, dumb beasts when they threaten his flock."

Goliath seemed amused. "Am I a yelping dog that you would scare me with a pebble? Come closer, little mouse, and when I'm done, there will not be enough left of you to feed the birds!"

David laughed. "You, Goliath, will supply them with a heartier meal!"

He whirled the two cords of the leather sling above his head, let go of one end, and launched the stone toward the grinning brute. It struck Goliath in the middle of his forehead. The giant staggered but remained standing. He lifted his hands to his still-smiling face, drew them back, and stared at the blood that pooled in his palms. He looked about in stunned, helpless disbelief. His eyelids fluttered and closed, and then he toppled, hitting the ground with a thunderous crash, like a huge felled tree in a cloud of dust.

The slaying of Goliath became a legend among the people, and David, in their eyes, the deliverer they had prayed for. Saul at first joined in their acclaim, hosting a huge banquet to celebrate David's valor, commissioning him as a general in his army. But as the excitement waned, my father's jealousy and suspicion took hold of him again.

He sent David into the most dangerous battles and when the young warrior returned successful, parading through the streets to the cheers of the crowds, Saul's insecurity turned to unreasoning hatred.

I tried to speak for my friend, but my father refused to hear me.

"He has the love of the people," he screamed. "What more can he desire except to be their king?"

"You cannot question his loyalty," I protested. "You have seen it. How many times has he deferred to your judgment? How many times has he obeyed your orders, unquestioningly? What evidence is there that he has been anything but another devoted son to you?"

Even as I offered these words in his defense, I recalled the sparkle in David's eyes as he spoke of his ambition. Was he plotting against the king? I loved him too much to believe it.

The complicated truth is that my father also loved David. But he couldn't allow himself to trust those feelings. He couldn't find a safe place for them in his tortured heart.

I had my own difficult feelings to face when the king approved of David's marriage to Michal, my sister. Would he no longer need me to confide in, to lean upon, to hold close in his sorrows and joys? Love and pain are intertwined. How do we sort out the strands of them?

What I learned in my brief life is that we must rescue what is noble from what is base, beginning within ourselves—something my father could never do.

He sent spies to follow David's every move and then to kill him as he slept. I was unaware of the plot. I still could not believe that my father meant to do harm to David.

But rumors reached my sister. That night, Michal arranged his bedclothes so that in the darkness they would appear as the sleeping form of her husband. When the spies came, asking to speak with David, she refused to let them into the room. "He is sick," she said. They peered around her at the bundled shape in the bed, suspicious but afraid to exceed their authority. Reluctantly, they returned to Saul for further instructions. It gave David the time he needed to make his escape.

I knew where he would go. To Samuel. I set out after him and the next day I found him in Ramah.

We embraced, in tears.

"Jonathan," he cried desperately, "What have I done? What is my sin that your father seeks my life?"

"It's not your sins but your virtues that enrage my father," I said. "You are the man, the leader, he can never be. He will try to disgrace you and slander you, but I'm sure he does not mean to kill you. In any case, I will protect you."

"Perhaps, you can," he said. "With your help, I can test his intentions. Tomorrow is the new moon and there will be a feast. I will be expected to sit at table with the king, but I will remain in hiding. When your father asks for me, say I have gone to Bethlehem—religious obligation, a yearly ritual sacrifice, family tradition. Study his reaction. If he is calm and understanding, I will believe that I can be safe in his presence. But if his countenance changes with anger and hatred, then, Jonathan, you and I will know his true motives and the danger that faces us both."

"I will do as you wish," I said. "But whatever happens, do not turn away from *me*."

David smiled. "Jonathan, I love you as I love my own soul. Nothing can change that."

"Remain in this place," I went on quickly. "When you are missed, I will return and shoot three arrows into the air. If I aim to the east, it will mean that all is well, to the west . . . I shall pray that we meet again."

At the feast, David's empty place was noticed but ignored at first. On the second day, however, the king questioned me, harshly. "Where is your friend, the great hero? What is the meaning of his absence, both yesterday and today?"

I repeated the story David and I had agreed upon. My father turned on me in rage.

"You son of a perverse, scheming woman! Do you think I can't see that you have chosen him over me, to your shame? Fool that you are, you do not see that his ascendancy is your downfall! As long as David lives, you will never be king! I am protecting *you*! Find the traitor, bring him to me, and he shall surely die!"

The truth was bitterly clear.

The next morning, I went to our appointed meeting place, raised my bow and shot three arrows into the air, aiming westward. I dismissed my servants and waited. In the distance David appeared, walking toward me, arms outstretched. Weighed down with unbearable sadness, we embraced, kissed, and wept.

"Go in peace," I said finally. "I know that God is between us forever." I never saw him again.

My father's mad jealousy increased and he continued to pursue David. His obsession was so complete that he neglected other matters and when the Philistines attacked once more, he was unprepared, his army in disarray.

The last battle took place on the plain of Jezreel, at the foot of

Mt. Gilboa. A Philistine archer's aim had been true and my father was badly wounded. I looked into his eyes and saw not fear but something far worse—utter despair. I knew, in that moment, that we would both die on that day.

I loved my father, in spite of all the hurt he had inflicted, and I pitied him for all the needless pain he had brought on himself. But neither love nor pity could unravel the cords of evil that bound him. I had been forced to be a disloyal son in order to be an honest man.

And David, made for great deeds and simple pleasures . . . David, with his talent for sparking minds and touching souls . . . David, my friend, my brother, I will meet you in another life where love and truth are one.

Abishag

I AM ABISHAG, the last concubine of King David, the comfort of his old age. Not a mistress in the way so many others had been, for when they brought me to him, he was barely alive— a pale, shivering, pitiful invalid. But I *was* chosen for my beauty.

I don't mean to be immodest. I had never been as pleased with my appearance as others seemed to be. If my skin was smooth and my features fair, it was, after all, no accomplishment on my part and it did not shield me from the ordinary struggles of life.

I was born in Shunem, a small village just south of Mount Tabor, near Nazareth. Nothing exciting happens in our town, though a story is told that once, long ago, the prophet Elisha passed through and took shelter in the home of a wealthy Shunamite family and that he raised their only son from the dead! It's a little hard to believe . . . because I've never known any wealthy people who live in Shunem!

My early life was strenuous but simple. We followed a routine, out of necessity. Being the oldest of seven children, I always had brothers and sisters to mind, to feed and amuse and keep out of trouble, in addition to my other chores—helping my mother with the baking, the cleaning, the laundry. It left little time for dreams, but mine were safely stored away for those precious moments when I could lie in my bed, bathed by moonlight, and imagine my future.

To be married to a good man, an important man, whose calling was to improve the world, to tackle evil and replace it with goodness. A man who would allow me to take part in a great cause, who would value my thoughts and trust my spirit. But, of course, no one I was likely to meet would measure up to my hopes. It remained a fantasy.

Until one day, a regiment of the king's soldiers rode into our village. They required water and food for their horses and for themselves. We busied ourselves providing for their needs. Their captain, a handsome young man named Benaiah, took his dinner in my home. He smiled at me as I served the meal and as he was leaving, he asked my name.

"Abishag," I whispered, bowing my head.

"Thank you, Abishag," he said. "Your hospitality has been most welcome. If I have occasion to return, I hope you will be here to greet me again."

That occasion came quickly. The next week, he was back and spent most of his time in private conversation with my father. Before I realized what was happening, I was engaged to be married!

Of course, I was nervous, but I could not help but be excited. A new life in a bustling big city! Parties and banquets to attend on the arm of my prominent husband. Perhaps even the chance to express my opinion about the latest political squabble or military campaign.

I had never been to Jerusalem and to a seventeen-year-old girl, it was a wonder. The buildings, markets, roads clogged with traffic, even the people seemed larger than life. My apprehensions were overcome by a sense of adventure.

My husband-to-be placed me in the home of his relatives, an elderly couple who treated me kindly and demanded little in return. Truthfully, I had almost no responsibilities at all, except to wait patiently while plans for the wedding were finalized. I was not consulted about this matter.

Over the next several weeks, I saw Benaiah infrequently—military obligations, he explained—though once he did escort me to a banquet at which I was introduced to some of the advisors to the King! I was certain I had made a poor impression but he reassured me sweetly.

Then, one evening, Benaiah arrived at the house where I was staying and led me outside to the garden. He appeared agitated, pacing, wringing his hands. It frightened me. Finally, he spoke.

"We cannot be married. I'm sorry, but it's impossible now."

The garden began to spin around me. "I don't understand," I stammered.

"A decision has been made," he said. "I dare not disobey."

"Decision?"

He stared at me with an expression of pain and anger.

"You have been chosen to be a . . . nurse for the King. They will come for you tomorrow. If only . . . ," he stopped himself. "It's out of my hands," he said. Then, he was gone.

The next morning, still dazed and numb with heartbreak. I was taken to the King's residence, bathed in scented oils, dressed in a garment of fine white linen, and brought to his chamber.

David struggled to raise himself on the bed, reached out to adjust the lamp on the stand to give more light, and motioned me forward. He lifted his frail hand, placed it on my cheek, and gazed silently at my face until tears came to his eyes.

It was not difficult to please him, as I soon learned. This man who had toppled a giant, ruled an empire, schemed and killed to satisfy his desires and increase his power, now wanted nothing more than to rest in the warmth of my arms. And talk.

Sometimes his mind was like a rickety wagon without a driver, wandering off the road, bumping over the rocks, tossing him about like a piece of baggage. But then, in the next moment, he'd find the reins and steer onto a path. He'd wave his hands as if clearing a mist before his eyes and speak in a steady voice. The story of his life—that's what he wanted to share with me. He must have realized that I was a safe listener with no part in the political intrigue that still swirled around him, even on his deathbed. I think too, as old and ill as he was, he couldn't resist trying to impress a beautiful woman.

Listening helped to distract me from my sorrow. In time, I came to look forward to each new chapter of the story, which he told very well. I experienced traces of the charm and vitality he must have exuded as a younger man. I was not called upon to comment. An occasional question or sympathetic nod of my head was enough to keep him going. I felt like an observer of great events of history, with the advantage of glimpsing the messy truth behind the public reports.

He had come to the throne at the age of thirty. The nation was divided, north and south, but David was determined to rule over *all* the people. For his capital, he chose Jerusalem—almost exactly on the border between the two kingdoms of Israel and Judah. To claim it, he cleared out the original inhabitants, the Jebusites, and called it "the city of David." *His* city!

He set about centralizing power, breaking down old tribal allegiances, insisting on a more personal loyalty—to himself! In a stroke of genius, uniting religious and political forces, he had the sacred ark of the covenant ceremonially transported to the new capital and he himself danced ecstatically before the processional. Throngs of people filled the streets, bowed down, and wept at the arrival of this great symbol of their faith and their nation.

I tried to imagine the tired old man before me as he was on that day—prancing, grinning, reveling in the attention of his people and his God. Flexing the muscles of his young, robust body, whirling, leaping, tumbling, and shouting with sheer joy until he was lifted to a higher plane as the roaring of the crowds seemed to fade to a gentle hum within his head and his spirit was released to play in the peaceful realm of eternity.

As he told me, this was a period of complete fulfillment, when his words, even his wishes, were law. When he could lie on his couch, sip wine, strum the lyre, and compose grateful psalms to the God who had so favored him.

". . . Know that God has set apart the godly . . . God hears when I call . . ."

When *he* called. He was so sure of being one of the godly.

"In peace," he sang, "I will lie down and sleep for thou, alone, O God, maketh me dwell in safety."

But the peace he sang of soon shattered. As usual, his troubles arose not from stirrings of the spirit but from longings of the flesh.

Bathsheba! Another beautiful woman!

He spied her from his rooftop as she bathed, spilling perfume from a clay jar into the water and onto her bare skin. I remember how he described the scene to me, with a sense of awe—and regret, for it proved to be a terrible turning point in his life.

She was married—something that did not concern him greatly. He wanted her. He summoned her. He took her. Two months later, she informed him that she was with child. *His* child.

The husband, Uriah, a Hittite and a soldier in David's army, had been away for a long time—far too long to have fathered this child with his wife. To cover his sin, David recalled Uriah and urged him to return home to his marital bed, but the soldier cited the ritual taboo for those preparing for war: abstinence from all physical relations.

One plan was foiled but David had another. He ordered Uriah to the front lines, where death was more than probable. The husband never returned.

David married Bathsheba. And then his great anguish began.

There were prophets in those days. They did not really tell the future. They told the *truth*. But it amounts to the same thing, one way or another. The truth *is* the future, isn't it?

The prophet Nathan was respected by David, so when he approached the King, he was sure to be heard and heeded. Nathan told David a fable:

> There was a rich man and a poor man. The poor man had only one beloved ewe who was like a daughter to him. One day, the rich man stole the ewe, killed it, and cooked it to feed a traveling stranger, even though the rich man had plenty of his own food to satisfy the hunger of his guest.

David was incensed by the tale. "It is a sin!" he cried. "A man who would do such a thing deserves to die!"

The prophet stared at him. "*You* are that man," he said. "You have earned the punishment of God. This is the curse of Yahweh: *'I will raise up evil against you, out of your own house.'* One child shall die, not even named. Another will turn against you— and, for all your pleading, will not be saved."

Absalom! David's third son would one day revolt and fight to gain his father's throne. David, forced to flee Jerusalem, would prevail in the end but before the final battle, he would beg his own soldiers to spare his son's life. David's wish was not to be granted. Absalom was killed.

I believe David never recovered. Lying beside me, so many years later, his desperate cry sounded still as painful as it must have been on the day he received the terrible news: "My son, my son, would I had died instead of you."

Such crushing defeat, as a father, as a husband, as a vulnerable, fallible man—in stark contrast to the all-knowing, all-powerful mask he wore as king—must have torn him apart. Even great rulers who alter history and receive the honor and praise of their people—as David did and *merited* in many ways—cannot necessarily count on happiness in their own lives.

In David's last years, the question of succession provoked fierce debate, plots, and counterplots. As he lay dying, his eldest son, Adonijah, declared himself king. Bathsheba, with the support and advice of Nathan, went to the bedridden monarch to remind him of his promise to elevate their son Solomon to the throne. David, with practically his last breath, was still powerful enough to make the decision. Solomon would be the next king of Israel. He was summoned to hear his father's final instructions. I observed their meeting from a corner of the room.

David began his speech as the wise statesman and faithful follower of Yahweh.

"I am about to go the way of all the earth," he said. "Be strong, my son, and show yourself a man. Care for the people. Care for the ways of our God. Walk in the commandments and testimonies of the Law of Moses and you will prosper in all you do, wherever you turn."

But he remained a politician to the last. With a final burst of ruthless anger, he commanded his son to exterminate all those who had betrayed the house of David.

David reigned thirty-three years. He died "full of days, riches, and honor" and was buried in Jerusalem.

I did not love him, but I had grown to care for him. In some strange way a bond had formed between us. My simple hopes had gone unfulfilled. His lofty ambitions had nearly all been realized. He had created an empire, extended its borders, and brought prosperity to the people. In the end, however, great deeds cannot create a contented soul. That must come from a higher ruler—the only One who can give life and grant peace.

Zadok

I AM ZADOK, high priest of Israel in its golden age, advisor to the great kings David and Solomon, and overseer of the most glorious temple ever conceived on earth. Faithfulness to Yahweh and loyalty to the nation formed my character and shaped my destiny, and God blessed me beyond all the hopes I ever held for myself.

As a young man, before I donned the priestly vestments, I fought in the royal wars on the side of David against Saul and was known as one who was "mighty in valor." I did not question Saul's legitimacy, only his stability. He was unacceptably flawed—jealous, petty, volatile. His downfall was inevitable. In David's eyes, I could read the future.

In those conflicts, I established a bond with the next king, for he too possessed extraordinary skill in battle and he admired my daring spirit. However, the role to which God called me was not military but religious. Since I traced my descent from Eleazar, the third son of Aaron, the brother of Moses, I was bound to uphold the Covenant as a priest.

When David established his kingship, he made the bold decision to rescue the ark of the covenant from the town of Baal-judah where it had been housed in obscurity and return it to Jerusalem. The ark was the most powerful symbol of our race and religion. It deserved to be enshrined at the heart of the nation, in the capital city.

I was serving God at the sanctuary in Gibeon when the King summoned me. It had been some years since we last met but he greeted me warmly. He told me of his plan and I affirmed his intention.

"I need your assistance," David said. "I must have someone I can trust as high priest."

"But, sire," I said. "Abiathar is high priest."

He smiled, waiting for me to understand. "Someone I can *trust,*" he repeated.

I nodded in silence, in awe at the enormity of his implications.

"After all," David continued cheerfully, "the duties of high priest are really too great for any one man. Better that they be shared—by one who knows Yahweh and another who knows Yahweh . . . and David!"

He paused, considering my reaction, which was only a numb blank stare.

"So, Zadok," he said. "You shall serve me with the same ardor you displayed as a warrior. With just as much courage as before, but, now, with a little more . . . worldly wisdom."

"I only hope to serve God," I said. "With all the courage and wisdom I am given."

"So do we all," David said, ending our conversation.

As a priest, I understood that I was to be the embodiment of the Covenant, the representative of Israel's union with God. Mosaic law declared that we were to be a "kingdom of priests" and a "holy nation." But it was clear in everyday experience that the nation was far from holy. Idolatry, infidelity, and injustice abounded. Priests became the substitute symbols of ideal purity, expected to *be* all that the people, in general, failed to be!

A threefold hierarchy existed within the priesthood: the Levites, responsible for the service of the sanctuary; the sons of Aaron, charged with the duties of preaching, teaching, and carrying out the sacrifices on the altar; and the high priest, the custodian of all past revelation, legal, and spiritual precedent. He alone, delegated by God, entered the holy of holies, once a year, to make atonement for the sins of *all* God's people! This was to be *my* responsibility!

Imagine the crushing weight laid upon my shoulders! Imagine the indescribable exhilaration with which I accepted it!

As formidable as my religious duties were, I had to face, in my time, even greater political struggles. Absalom, David's son, was plotting to steal the hearts of the people and his father's throne. He succeeded in gathering such a large following that David was forced to flee from Jerusalem. Before his departure, the king gave me his instructions.

"Zadok," he said. "This is a God-given test of faith. If Yahweh is on my side, I will return to the city in triumph. If not . . . well, may God be merciful to us all. Trust and pray, my friend."

The final, terrible battle took place in Ephraim. The rebel forces were conquered and Absalom—in spite of his father's pleas for clemency—was killed. David was stunned by the loss of his son. His broken heart, I believe, never healed. But there were yet more tragedies to come, centering around another son, Adonijah, and the question of succession to the throne.

Years later, old and ill, on his deathbed, David still had power enough to decide which of his sons would succeed him as king. Adonijah, assuming his royal inheritance prematurely, had the backing of Abiathar and Joash, the commander of the army. With Nathan the prophet, I stood behind Solomon, Bathsheba's son. The spell that Bathsheba had cast over David had never been broken. Even at the end, she was able to rouse him and manipulate his will. In this case it served our common purpose. With whispers and kisses, she reminded David of his promise to name Solomon as his heir and sufficiently revived him so that he rose from his bed, called for his counselors, and issued what proved to be his final command.

"Zadok," he said, as I entered his bedchamber, "this day you shall anoint Solomon king of Israel. He shall ride upon my own mule, down to the spring of Gihon beneath the city. There you shall pour oil upon his forehead and declare him keeper of the Covenant. Trumpets shall blow and the people shall cry, 'Long live King Solomon!'"

Adonijah and his supporters were feasting in celebration of their apparent success. The blare of trumpets interrupted and spoiled their party. They understood at once the meaning of that sound. Adonijah's supposed friends suddenly scurried as if someone had thrust a torch into a nest of vermin. The pitiful pretender was left alone with a handful of grapes and a mouthful of wine to experience the bitter end of his brief dream. He ran directly to the sanctuary and threw himself upon the altar weeping pathetically, waiting, almost gratefully, for the sword of justice to descend, pleading for mercy in a tortured voice that no one but Yahweh could hear in the empty, echoing space.

I heard. I *saw*. I watched, at a distance, as that slumping, sobbing figure tensed and turned to face his judgment.

Solomon appeared. Supremely confident in the knowledge of his newly bequeathed authority, he approached the altar with majestic stride.

"Adonijah!" he called. "You are a traitor! You deserve to die!"

Solomon moved closer until he was standing over his whimpering rival. He reached down and took Adonijah's face in his hands.

"But you are also the *son of my father*! My *brother* . . . the kinship—embarrassing as it is to me—moves me to spare your life for now, as long as you remain out of my sight, out of my hair! One step, one *tiny* step, into my life henceforth and I will have to include you in my prayers for the dead!"

Adonijah accepted the reprieve but he did not learn its lesson. Not long afterward, he offended the King once again and was killed. At about that same time, Solomon conducted a purge of all former resisters still involved in the government—military, political, and spiritual leaders. Abiathar, because of his position as high priest, was let off easily, banished to his ancestral home of Anathoth, with the same warning Solomon had issued to his brother: stay out of my way and stay out of public scrutiny. Unlike Adonijah, Abiathar complied with the terms of his exile.

With Abiathar gone, I became the high priest. No longer *sharing* that momentous responsibility, but taking it upon my *own* shoulders. My dream had come true.

Solomon had inherited a large empire, extending from cities in Egypt to the desert sands of Syria. The young king, whom, I think, his supporters had expected to control, turned out to be a shrewd and sensible ruler. He understood the reality of this new form of government, with its offices and departments, its administrative functionaries. He divided the nation into twelve districts, roughly equal in size and resources, but unrelated to the old tribal boundaries. There were officers for food, agriculture, taxes, civic maintenance, law enforcement, and military matters. The requirements of the royal court were astounding. In a single day, the King demanded more than five hundred bushels of flour and meal, ten oxen, twenty cattle, one hundred sheep, plus a remarkable amount of fowl and grain and vegetables to feed his entourage. Not to mention singers, dancers, musicians, and poets to entertain them.

Solomon himself possessed boundless energy. He wrote songs and proverbs, studied trees, birds, architecture, and was capable of discussing an innumerable variety of subjects with knowledge and insight. He took a new wife almost every month, it seemed.

Many of these marriages were designed to seal alliances with other nations—Moab, Edom, Phoenicia, Egypt. For her dowry, the Pharaoh's daughter offered the entire city of Gezer! It is said that Solomon had more than seven hundred wives and three hundred concubines! Perhaps a slight exaggeration, even for such a legendary lover!

His foreign brides brought with them their own religious beliefs and Solomon allowed them great latitude to continue in their alien cultic practices. Indeed, he built shrines and sanctuaries for their gods, imported pagan priests to enact their rituals, and even *participated* in them. He crossed the line between tolerance and idolatry. That sin, above all others, would lead to his downfall.

But in the beginning, no one—myself included—chose to raise an objection. The problem was simply overshadowed by the great project—the building of the Temple! The indiscretions of a king? An old story! But the Temple was something utterly, miraculously new!

We commenced in the month of Ziv, the second month of the fourth year of Solomon's reign. The King commissioned Hiram of Tyre as chief architect. The Phoenicians were the great builders of our day, and we would settle for nothing less than the most skillful craftsmen for our holy work. We chose Mt. Moriah for the site. We drew up the initial construction plan, calculated resources, considered the transportation of materials and ways to cover the huge expenses involved. Then we focused on the most immediate challenge of all—inspiring the unqualified devotion of the people.

Solomon would institute a forced labor program that applied to all foreign slaves. But, in itself, the program would not establish a sufficient work force to accomplish the task. Our own people would have to join in the effort. A law was devised whereby any able-bodied citizen might be drafted to serve one month out of every three. We had to create a vision of the majestic results that would issue from their toil. We had to keep their minds set on the grandeur and glory of this incomparable edifice that was to be the house of *their* God! Despite a certain amount of inevitable resistance and rather mild grumbling among the populace, the plan succeeded.

Some thirty thousand people were conscripted and sent to labor camps to fell the cedars of Lebanon, which were turned into rafts and floated on the sea to their destination. Another eighty thousand workers went into the stone quarries. Seventy thousand more sweated and strained as haulers.

The Temple took seven years to build. As each stage of the structure arose, the people grew more and more mesmerized by its beauty and its immensity. By the time of its completion, the nation vibrated with a sense of wonder and gratitude.

The outer walls of the Temple were ten feet thick. Ten steps led to the entrance, which was framed by two gleaming pillars of bronze. In the expansive outer courtyard stood a huge bronze bowl resting on twelve bronze oxen for the cleansing ritual and, off to the right, a great marble altar for the animal sacrifices. The interior, sixty feet long and thirty feet across, had a cypress floor with the star of David inlaid at its center. The walls of cedar were adorned with intricate carvings in ivory and gold. Sunlight entered dimly through a series of windows placed just below the roof beams. At the far end of this chamber, behind a small wooden altar, a single door led to the Holy of Holies—a room without windows, thirty feet square, in which the ark would be placed, guarded by two winged cherubim carved of olivewood and plated with gold.

When, at last, the day of the dedication ceremony arrived, Solomon called an assembly of the elders, the heads of the tribes, religious leaders, government officials, and all the people of Israel. The priests and Levites, in procession, carried the sacred vessels and implements and, going before them, I held the two stone tablets of the law that Moses had received from God.

Solomon stood before the altar, raised his hands to heaven, and prayed: "O God of Israel, there is no God like you, above the earth or upon it, keeping your promise and proving your infinite love for us, your chosen ones who walk humbly before you."

He paused for a moment, then raised his voice dramatically, "But will God indeed dwell on earth?"

In our hearts, we answered silently. "Yes! God will dwell on earth! In this temple!"

"O my God," the king continued his prayer, "hear the cry of your servant Solomon and the supplication of your people Israel, that you may be pleased by looking upon this place to which you have given your name."

The feast that followed lasted seven days. It seemed that all our prayers had been answered.

In time, we descended from this peak of ecstasy to the hard ground of reality. Pride in the power of our king and our nation gave way to anger at increased taxes, restrictive laws, the loss of autonomy, the widening gap between the poor and the rich, government's disdain for common farmers and merchants and its infatuation with the moneyed elite.

Solomon's kingdom grew top-heavy. Desperate, in debt, he was forced to hand over to Hiram twenty cities in Galilee. The confidence and support of his people withered. Opposition moved him to greater arrogance. He built more shrines to pagan gods. He himself bowed down before them and encouraged his subjects to do the same. Solomon had forgotten his own proverb: "It is an abomination for kings to do evil, for the throne is established by righteousness."

Solomon reigned for forty years and left chaos behind him. But he also left us the Temple! My descendants would continue in the priesthood for more than three hundred years, until the Temple itself was destroyed by invading armies.

God works wonders through us in spite of our flaws and faithlessness, in spite of our stubbornness and sin. It is true in every age. In every age, the people call upon God to right the wrongs of the world, but hesitate to see themselves as God's agents on earth. At the most critical times, we fail to report for duty. God goes on saving and redeeming, but can you imagine, for a moment, how life might flow smoothly and peacefully toward its true destiny if only we surrendered our destructive human willfulness to the loving divine will? When that truth finally conquers our hearts, we will know that God indeed dwells on earth!